THE ALLEGORY OF QUEST
A Study in Arthur Miller's Plays

THE ALLEGORY OF QUEST
A Study in Arthur Miller's Plays

Satyendra Kumar

KALPAZ PUBLICATIONS
Delhi-110052

The Allegory of Quest : A Study in Arthur Miller's Plays

Rs. 680

ISBN: 81-7835-276-1

Published in 2004 in India by
Kalpaz Publications,
C-30, Satyawati Nagar, Delhi-110052
E-mail : Kalpaz@hotmail.com

Laser Typesetting at : Shree Vaishnavi Creations, Delhi
Printed at : Mehra Offset Press, Delhi

To
My father, Late Deo Kumar P Sharma
with grateful regards

Contents

Foreword 9

Preface 11

1. **The Theatre of Everyman** **17**
2. **The Island and The Continent (All My Sons)** **69**
3. **The American Myth** **93**
4. **The Crisis of Conscience** **117**
5. **Betrayal and Sacrifice** **137**
6. **The Shifting Camera** **177**
7. **The Allegory of Quest** **207**

Bibliography 217

Index 229

Foreword

It is indeed a delightful experience to write the foreword of the book entitled *The Allegory of Quest: A Study in Arthur Miller's Plays* by Mr. Satyendra Kumar. The book is consummately-crafted cogently illustrated perceptive exploration into the crusts of Miller's dramatic tenor from the specific perspective of the quest motive which forms the matrix of experience in Miller's drama. To tell the truth the whole range of modern drama of the Western world is a search for a meaningful stance against the panorama of immense anarchy and futility. Modern theatre is an allegory of quest where the protagonist is everyman embodying the contemporary struggle of modern man who is groping en route in the labyrinths of life and reality. The book analyses the plays of Miller threadbare throwing light on many unlit comers showing how Miller addresses himself to the world in which he lived but goes beyond it to the universal human condition and attains a metaphysical dimension Jonesco the famous dramatist was right when he remarked that since the artist apprehends reality directly he is a true philosopher. And it is the broadness, the depth, the sharpness, of his philosophical vision his living philosophy which determines his greatness. The present book spells out in most lucid terms the basic vision of the dramatist who fascinated the world with play after play and seized the dramatic stage for portraying the modern man's dilemma, the conflict between despair and hope between drift and purpose and produced a theatre of purpose like the great Greeks.

The book also makes full cognizance of the structural strategy developed by Miller to provide befitting mould to his tragic vision. Miller has synthesized varying tools and techniques coming out from different art and fine art forms. The book helps the readers see the real blending of motive and mould in his plays.

I am sure the book is immensely useful, and delightfully readable as it has been written in a see-through style with clarity of perception and competence of articulation.

Hari Mohan Prasad

Preface

Although there are numerous studies devoted to Miller's social realism, tragic vision and craftsmanship, very few attempts have been made to focus on the allegorical aspects of his plays.

This volume is a modest attempt at understanding Miller's dramatic corpus as an allegory of quest, as an appropriate structure for a moral exploration of modern man's dilemma. It is primarily addressed to the teachers and students of American literature and makes no claim to originality, except, perhaps, of emphasis on a less-touched upon aspect of Miller's dramatic genius.

In fact, I owe much to all Miller scholars as I have drawn materials and ideas heavily from them. However, occasionally, I have ventured to record my personal response to verious aspects of Miller's dramaturgy.

The methodology in this volume is intended to be inductive. The ideas set forth in the introductory chapter entitled 'The Theatre of Everyman' are, in fact, proposed as a thesis to be explored rather than as assumptions which the reader is asked to take on faith.

The first chapter examines the growth of modern

drama in a historical perspective beginning from Henrik Ibsen to Arthur Miller. The allegorical framework offers Miller an artistic opportunity to search for identity and examine the tragic consequences of failure and guilt in the American society.

The second chapter 'The Island and the Continent' examines 'All My Sons' in detail. The play evokes the problem of acceptance of social responsibility which helps it achieve the dignity of a Greek tragedy. The hero Keller represents social consciousness and his journey from self to non-self makes the end of his quest.

The third chapter 'American Myth is an analysis of Miller's masterpiece 'Death of a Salesman'. Willy Loman's tragedy symbolises the inevitable misfortune of our own times. Man's search for 'personal dignity' forms a significant aspect of the play. The play anatomises the failure of man to be himself, to be 'something' or 'somebody' to be a 'success' in life. The play tells us what it means to be a human being in this treacherous cosmos. Finally, bewildered by the failure and futility of his life, Loman goes bravely to his death still deceiving himself. However, his predicament gives him heroic stature in this tragedy of modern times.

The fourth chapter 'The Crisis of Consience' examines Miller's 'crucible'. The play utilises history as allegory to portrary the cold war scene in America in which the impact of the committee to investigate unAmerican activities resulted in fear and mistrust. Miller, in fact, pays homage to the martyrdom of the fearless men and women for the freedom of conscience.

In the fifth chapter 'Betrayal and Sacrifice', the conflict between the individual agonies and the social values of ethical code is stressed in Miller's other plays like 'A Memory of Two Mondays', 'A View from the Bridge', 'After the Fall' and 'Incident at Vichy'.

The sixth chapter 'The Shifting Camera' is a study in the dramatic technique of Miller who made the most of the realistic, expressionistic and rhetorical techniques in a bid to reveal life in its various facets and search for human motives.

The last chapter 'The Allegory of Quest', which brings the main thrust of the present study to a sharp focus, examines the semantic and technical aspects of the motive of quest in modem European and American drama which Miller inherited.

Each chapter demonstrates how the quest motive contributes functional attitudes and allegorical patterns to the action of the play.

The present volume was, in fact, begun as a doctoral dissertation for a Ph.D. degree of Magadh University (Bihar) under the direction of Prof. Hari Mohan Prasad, Head of the department of English of the same University. Dr. Prasad's superior critical acumen was matched by his thoughtful consideration in suggesting a fresh, new direction to my research pursuit. Without his help, this study might not have seen the light of day.

I am very much indebted to a number of other persons for giving me valuable guidance and encouragement in the preparation of this book. I would like to make particular mention of Dr. Shaileshwar Sati Prasad, former Head of the department of English, Patna University and Dr. S.C. Singh, Associate Professor of English, University of Rajasthan, Jaipur for encouraging me to get my doctoral dissertation published in a book form.

I am also greatly indebted to some of my old University chums including Mr. M. Shakeel Ahmad, I.A.S., Mr. M.K. Sinha, I.P.S., Mr. Washir Ahmad, I.P.S., Dr. U.N. Singh, Assistt. Commissioner, Kendriya Vidyalay Sanghatan, Patna and Prof. B.K. Tripathi for their stimulating suggestions.

Giving adequate expression to my indebtedness to my relatives, Mr. Madan Sharma and his wife Meena, Mr. Surendra Sharma and Mr. Kaushal Kumar, all living in New York, is rather a difficult task. I am grateful to all of them for sending me valuable reference books and other related materials as and when I needed them.

I am equally grateful to a host of other colleagues and well-wishers including Dr. Madan Mohan Pd. Singh Prof. Aquil Ahmad, Dr. Madan Prasad Sinha of S.N. Sinha College pro Jehanabad, Dr. Lallan Pd. Singh of college of commerce Patna, Dr. Ajay Kumar, noted Neurologist, Patna, Mr. H. Rehman, Indian Information service officer, Gaya, Mr. Sanjay Kumar, Director, Ankur Public School, Patna and Mr. Nageshwar Pd. Singh of my native village Kosdihra, who have been, in fact, a great source of inspiration to me in the preparation of this book.

To my principal, Dr. Chandra Bhushan Sharma, I owe a special debt of gratitude for, constant encouragement and support.

I am also thankful to Mr. Pramod Kumar, Advocate, proprietor of M/s Vedant Computers, Jehanabad for having done an excellent job of typing the manuscript.

Last but not the least, I must put on record my

very special gratitude to Mr. Amit Garg, for bringing out the book with such promptness and in such an excellent format.

Satyendra Kumar

1

The Theatre of Everyman

No man is an island, entire of itself ;
every man is a piece of the continent,
a part of the main...
any man's death diminishes me,
because I am involved in mankind,
and therefore never send to know
for whom the bell tolls; it tolls for thee,

—*John Donne*

The main body of modern drama begins as a response to the revolutionary speculations and promptings of the second half of the 18th century. An idealistic school arises that acclaims aspiration, the principle of liberty and its associated ideals. It goes under the name of 'romanticism'. Its essential promptings continue to prevail in the theatre long after the specific romantic technique and style have changed substantially. The second half of the 18th century was the age of Rousseau and his followers. They opposed the claims of nature to those of a frozen, polished society, and acclaimed the equality of man and his essential goodness and perfectibility. It was the age of Voltaire who applied the dynamite of rationalism to the concrete of established religion and government. In the American Revolution and in the French Revolution of 1789 the common people saw the beginning of a democratic dispensation. The masses were fired by the ideals of 'liberty, equality and fraternity'.

As Western Europe becomes a predominantly middle-class world that busies itself with practical matters and commonplace interests, its playwrights begin to grapple with realities instead of favouring romantic dreams. The result is the realism—that distinguishes a major portion of the drama from the beginning of the pre-romantic era to the present day. A vast and troubled life, inseparable from the travails and aspirations of modernity, unfolds before the dramatists of Europe and America. Many of them try to face it bravely and intelligently. In trying to project it effectively from the stage, moreover, the playwrights experiment with styles that carry them well beyond realism, too. Modern theatre, of which Romanticism is the seedbed, becomes, then, a richly varied enterprise of realism, on one hand, and of numerous departures from it, on the other.

Henrik Ibsen is justly called the 'father of modern drama.' Ibsen wrote his first realistic social drama *Pillars of Society* in 1877. John Gassner calls Ibsen "a viking of the modern drama standing at the prow of his tilted boat with the sea widening before him."[1] His work is precisely a voyage of adventures, depredations and explorations. At first we find him in his native Norway, his blood boiling with desire for open sea. He pursues a profession, studies at the university and enters the narrow theatre of his day. This is the period of his mild romantic plays. Then suddenly he "swoops down upon the settlements of the slumbering bourgeoisie. He burns their "doll's houses" and loud outcries from those whom he has rudely evicted."[2] This is the period of his *Pillars of Society, Doll's House, Ghosts,* and *Enemy of the People.* According to Gassner, "Like all great writers Ibsen was a warrior, a voyager, and the upshot of his struggle is a noble body of drama which expresses modern man."[3]

In the course of both grappling with realities and sometimes evading them in his own peculiar way, Ibsen inaugurated— important modifications in modern dramatic practice. More than any of his immediate predecessors, Ibsen discards[3] at long last the 'well-made play' of graduated intrigues and obvious plotting which Scribe and his followers had put on the market in the nineteenth century. He wrote a number of plays that gave the illusion of undistorted reality. Those plays enabled the playgoer to observe the characters and ponder over the ideas or implications of a drama instead of watching the gyrations of plot. As a matter of fact, Ibsen did not actually invent the drama of ideas, he only assured its triumph in the modern world. He did this by applying himself boldly to ideas of broad relevance to man and society and by projecting them in defiance of conventional taboos.

For all his superficially provincial tendencies and despite the small-town backgrounds of many of his plays, he possessed something of the largeness of spirit that is to be found among the Greeks and the Elizabethans as well as among the great romanticists.

> The bold creativeness of Shakespeare and Goethe is sporadically present in the totality of his output, echoes of

> 'Faust' resound in 'Brand' and 'Peer Gynt' and 'Euripides' frontal attack on convention as well as the Euripidean retrospective technique, pulsates in Ibsen's works.[4]

When Ibsen left Norway in 1864 to begin his great epic dramas in Rome, the scientific Naturalism prefigured by Galileo, Bacon and Descarts had already triumphed. Darwin's *Origin of Species* which appeared in 1859, dealt a mortal blow at the divine origin of mankind. In the same year, Karl Marx had completed his 'Critique of Political Economy', a mechanistic approach to history which analysed the development of cultures solely on the basis of class interests. In 1863, Ŗenan published his *Life of Christ* in which Jesus was denied his divine birth, his miracles and his resurrection. Jesus was characterised less as a supernatural being than as an inspired prophet and rebel.

By the second half of the nineteenth century, naturalism was replacing supernaturalism, the experiment was superceding the apparition. The statistic was being substituted for the insight, prose was supplanting poetry. Religious orthodoxy was still powerful but the church had become the prey of hypocritical observances and superficial respectability. Science was growing arrogant and assured but did not provide any magical ideas or metaphysical grace to satisfy mankind's yearning for ritual and sanctity. The great social-political revolutions resulted in the consolidation of middle-class power. The failure of the radical revolution of 1813 had discouraged hopes that this power would be easily overthrown. Liberty, equality and fraternity were becoming cant terms. Wage slavery replaced serfdom. Justice was being corrupted by privilege. Progress was paying for its blessings with the evils of industrialism—slag heaps, child labour, blackened cities. The revolutionaries of the early nineteenth century had anticipated the full realization of human freedom. But the deterministic sciences put limits on man's possibilities. The machine broke his link with nature and his fellow beings. The state was beginning to make increasingly greater claims on his person. Modern man was stalked by chaos :

> Things fall apart, the centre cann't hold, Mere anarchy is loosed upon the world.[5.]

The image of modern society becomes of a dungeon-grey, filthy, squalid, forbidding— where man labours interminably, in the poisoned air at humiliating tasks.

The modern drama, in short, rides in on the second wave of Romanticism—not the cheerful optimism of Rosseau, with his emphasis on institutional reform but rather the dark fury of Nietzsche, with his radical demands for a total transformation of man's spiritual life. According to Robert Brustein, Nietzsche remains the most seminal philosophical influence on the theatre of revolt, the intellect against which almost every modern dramatist must measure his own."[6] When Nietzsche declared the death of God, he declared the death of all traditional values as well. Man could create new values only by becoming God. The only alternative to nihilism lay in revolt. Nietzsche's arrogant 'I will' was a desperate response to an absurd universe. And all modern revolt, as Albert Camus in his monumental study 'The Rebel' says, is "born of the spectacle of irrationality, confronted with an unjust and incomprehensible condition." Confronted with the same metaphysical absurdity, the modern dramatist takes up Nietzsche's challenge, assuming an attitude of refusal which puts him in conflict with the laws of modern necessity. Rejecting God, church, community and family— vindicating the rights of the individual against the claims of government, morality, conventions and rules—he adopts the posture of the rebel, chafing against restraints, determined to make all barriers crack.

Instead of examining the relationship between man and God, the social dramatists concentrates on man in society, in conflict with community, government, academy, church or family. Though the social drama is occasionally expressionistic, it is more frequently written in the realistic or Naturalistic style, through which the objective ideal is best maintained :

> Messianic voluptuousness and exuberance are replaced by more controlled and modulated feelings : social, political, moral and economic questions are aired in an atmosphere of impartiality. Sociological and Psychological insights grow common, scientific ideas begin to influence the dramatist, particularly Darwin's theory of heredity and environment. Ibsen, Strindberg, Shaw and Brecht all begin to think of themselves as literary scientists under the influence of Darwin, Lamarck or Marx.[7]

With Ibsen, the theatre made a revolutionary break with the past and that with Strindberg it went into a timeless world. Under the influence of Ibsen, the playwrights have shifted their attention from the external to the individual's interior world. They have tried to delineate human passions instead of the history of persons and their achievements. Strindberg has gone a step further in that he probed the human psyche and presented the aberrations in human character. Breaking the barrier between the normal and the abnormal, he has shown that the insane or the schizoid may be more rational than the so-called normal man or woman. Neurosis is no longer a disease of the mind but something born in reaction to the irrationality of existence.

The First World War had been pointless and agonizing. It did not even seem to have made war any less likely once the terms of the Treaty of Versailles had been announced. To the radicals' amazement and disgust the old system of unrestrained capitalism appeared to have survived the explosion in every country except Russia. German radicals including the playwright Ernst Toller, were in jail for their part in the Munich uprising of 1919. Their American counterparts had high hopes of some degree of socialism from Woodrow Wilson but by 1920 the Republican Harding had become president and big business was again in the saddle. The post-war generation was left disillusioned. The world looked like a wilderness. The result was "the Jazz age, the vicious whirling of the Bright young people, hectically gay to cover up the emptiness."[8]

The 1930's stand out from the whole history of the theatre as the decade of political theatre. It was the depression which brought about the change. In the boom days the politically minded writers had felt themselves to be voices crying in a spiritual wilderness. In the thirties, when millions were reduced by poverty and unemployment to an animal level of existence, they were urged to act. 'Power is People', concludes Lawson's 'Machine Song' (1937).

With the outbreak of the Second World War, the emphasis changed. The nations had now taken the step into action and the individual is caught up in it willy-nilly. From now on the emphasis is on him. Nowhere does his predicament press harder on him than in the drama of occupied France.

The thirties produced a theatre calling for action. The forties concentrated on the individual caught up in the action and the post-war theatre was left with all the emphasis on the individual because the action and the need for it, had passed.

The period from 1880 to 1930 is regarded as the age of experiment, the true hey-day of avant-gardisme. In these years the grounds of the theatre was stretched to their utmost limits and sometimes beyond. However ridiculous the result, theory was carried to the extreme in every direction. The microscopic was reached in a play of Austin Strong's in which the stage represented the inside of a man's skull and the macroscopic in dramas of social revolution, such as Hauptmann's *The Weavers,* where an entire class is the protagonist. Capek's *Adam the Creator* and Shaw's *Back to Methuselsh* both spanned the whole of mankind's development. Strindberg and Cocteau wrote plays with only one speaking character. The expressionists were using fantastic means to portray the crazy logic of men's souls, while the Naturalists were concerned with the outer semblance of reality. Yeats wanted his verse plays to be performed on a rug at one end of an ordinary room. The Dadaists invented a form of theatre which included throwing things at the audience.

Man's faith in all accepted values was entirely shaken in the twentieth century. He lost his faith in entirety and no longer did he bother about immortality. Having lost its centre, the absolute, human life became peripheral and relative. Hence alienation from God and society became the dominant theme of modern literature.

Ibsen had to cut all his romantic moorings before he could usher in the modern drama. Ibsen embarked upon an investigation of modern man and society which stamps his major contributions to the theatre. His *Brand* made a deep impression upon the consciousness of the liberal sixties, which teemed with ideas of liberation and witnessed the abolition of serfdom in Russia and of slavery in America. *The Pillars of Society* propounded the idea that society was founded on corruptions and lies. In *A Doll's House* Ibsen addressed himself to woman's place in society. He called upon women to come out into the world. Nora's leaving her house and children sounded incredibly outrageous at first sight. *Ghosts* is the tragedy of Mrs. Alving whose observance of the conventions of marriage bound her to a wayward and syphilitic husband. It startled the world by introducing the subjects of heredity and venereal disease into the theatre. But, in fact, Ibsen was only responding to the ferment of the age of Darwin and the naturalism of Emile Zola. Ibsen had already suggested the problem of the hereditary taint in *A*

Doll's House, when Helmer warned Nora against the heritage of dishonesty which she may pass on to her children. Broadly conceived, then, *Ghosts* combines the bleakest realism with an intense protest against everything that shackles the individual in his pursuit of happiness and integrity. *An Enemy of the People* is telling in its mockery of the complacencies and hypocrisies of respectable society which is willing to countenance anything for the sake of a profit : *The Wild Duck* is notable for its combination of reality and poetry. Being at heart a poet, Ibsen lacked the capacity for permanent adjustment to realism. Once, more he turned to the open sea of poetic adventure. His last works are with one exception, permeated with longing for a life of courageous freedom and revolt against compromise. Perhaps the fear of old age overcame him and sharpened his thirst for self-realization.

Ibsen's spirit brooded upon the theatre and brought forth a progeny that multiplied itself prodigiously. One Ibsenite, that Aristophanes of modernity whom no one will fall to identify as Bernard Shaw, equalled his master's stature and one antagonistic scandinavian Strindberg. Strindberg was his equal in genius, if not in execution. Ibsen's realism over Europe was a process rather than a static fait accompli, and most of the new playwrights did not follow a straight line. As a matter of fact, the drama traced a triple course in their work. At first it still worked in the romantic tradition, then it adopted realism and finally it swung away from literal realism and turned to imaginative or 'symbolic' drama. Still in most instances, their lasting work belongs to the realistic theatre. It was through realism that they were most closely allied with the promptings of their age and achieved the broadest intensities of experience and illumination.

The writer who attained greater intensities than Ibsen and carried his realistic art further than anyone in the North was August Strindberg. Ibsen's influence may be traced in Strindberg's *Lucky Pehr.* In this Swediah *Peer Gynt,* Strindberg opened a vein of social satire in the Swedish drama. Strindberg wrote a striking series of short stories on modern matrimony entitled *Married.* With its publication Strindberg laid the groundwork for his major contribution to the theatre. Here were all the familiar elements of Strindbergian drama : with ultra-realistic observation, psychological excoriation and anti-feminism. The gist of his thesis was that between man and woman there exists a constant and consuming struggle for power. Like D.H. Lawrence, Strindberg maintained that someone must be the master in marriage, and that the power was far less likely to be abused by men than women. One year after *Married,* in 1887, appeared *The Father*—one of the most gripping psychological dramas of the modern theatre. Title of play was likewise devoted to the danger of allowing a woman to deplete a man's strength. In both his full-length plays and one-acters, Strindberg proved himself a master of psychological conflict, as well as an unflinching painter of the realities which the so-called naturalists often confined to the surface of life. He had the talent for piercing the surface of things. He ranks with such master psychologists of modern literature as Tolstoy, Dostoyevsky and D.H. Lawrence. If he lacked Ibsen's largeness of spirit, he possessed more depth and intensity. Strindberg's symbolist plays like *The Damascus, The Dream Play* and *The Spook Sonata* are full of compassion for bedevilled mankind. They provide "a surrealist experience that perturbs the soul and opens windows in it without quite communicating with the mind."[9]

In the theatre, Strindberg becomes the forerunner of the expressionistic stage which widened dramatic horizons. Strindberg's symbolic plays have intrinsic merits because they are born of a probing, intense intellect and an infinite sensitivity to the pain of existence. His expressionist plays possess numerous incisive symbolizations of both the external and inner world of modern man.

Luigi Pirandello was an important figure in modern drama. His was a highly modern mind replete with the relativistic philosophy and psychiatric science of the twentieth century. The social and political realities which had forced themselves into the modern theatre received scant attention from him and the situations which he favoured most are remote from the cardinal conflicts of his age. Nevertheless, both his disillusionment and his psychology stamp him as an ultra-modern. A streak of naturalism appeared in Pirandello in his early works and it is present even in many of his most cerebral efforts. They present sordid situations and deal with elemental passions. Incest, prostitution and suicide appear liberally in *Six Characters in Search of an Author.* His first disillusionment with society came when he grew tired of political corruption and social hypocrisy. Thereafter he came to regard the state with those anarchistic suspicious which coloured many of his plays and determined his continual satirization of social conventions, especially of so-called respectability.

Pirandello's works remain a monument to the questioning and self-tormenting human intellect which is at war not only with the world, the flesh and the devil but also with its own limitations. Once the intellect has conquered problem after problem without solving the greatest question of all—namely, whether it is real itself rather than illusory—it reaches an impasse. Pirandello is the poet of that impasse. He is also the culmination of centuries of intellectual progress which have failed to make life basically more reasonable or satisfactory. He ends with a question mark. The drama, which is perhaps the oldest of the arts, began with the question "How shall we exist?" Logically after three thousand years of human effort to solve this first problem—it might therefore and with the question "Do we exist at all?" "But the drama has always been a faith rather than argument, and it has sought to provide an answer that would strengthen the spirit for its continual battle with the 'Everlasting Nay' that grins at us in a thousand shapes."

Oscar Wilde and Bernard Shaw descended upon England when the British drama was a fen of Philistine abominations. Bernard Shaw has been the modern world's most thorough playwright since he has played with everything. Having come to London, Shaw turned to social philosophy. He keenly observed and thought over the Victorian conflict between religion and science, the education of women, 'Mill on Liberty', the controversies over Darwinism and the philosophy of Spencer. The importance of the 'economic basis' which he was later to introduce as a major contribution to the content of modern English Drama suddenly dawned on him. This occurred in 1882 in a period of economic crisis which created a revival of interest in socialism. Shaw therefore studied socialist literature and allowed Marx to make 'a man' of him, as he declared in later years.

According to John Gassner, "Shaw added to his cloth Schopenhauer's concept of the world as 'Will', Neitzsche's faith in the evolution of man into superman, Lamarck's and Bergson's theories of evolution, Ibsen's plea for uninhibited self-realization and various other continental fabrics. Shaw gave the world of modern science and sociology a comedy commensurate with its intellectual scope. . . and for all his so-called clowning, his writings are permeated with a dignity that stems equally from an unintimidated mind and a noble spirit. Combined with his prefaces, his plays comprise a body of literature greater perhaps than any that has appeared in English since Shakespeare.

When America discovered through O'Neill and his successors that the theatre was an art and not an industry, drama became one of its richest natural resources. In both grief and gladness, the American dramatist was distinctly vital and energetic. This vitality was in fact as natural as breathing to the writers of the new world. It was inherent in the great era of American expansion. It could only find a proper stimulus when the nation found itself in a favoured position between 1918 and 1929 as the creditor of the world and its citizens looked forward to unlimited material progress. Whether the playwright accepted or resented this development, he shared its energy and exhibited it in his work.

O'Neill, like every significant writer, was not the product of merely theatrical developments or impulses. He was a veritable seismograph of the ideas, viewpoints and promptings of the new age. He reflected a general discontent with a materialistic America on the part of the younger creative sons of the age, a sense of frustration, a general straining for enriched experience and an assimilation of European thought and dramatic art. He responded to these underground stirrings and rumblings with crude but impressive intensity. In him Europe and America interbred, the one providing the chromosomes of thought and experience, the other the genes of grappling vitality.

O'Neill has caught the reality of common people living on sea or land. He has presented humanity struggling against inherited or acquired limitations and facing racial prejudice, poverty, the hardness of a stony soil, the frustrations of puritanism and the effects of a materialistic world which thwarts or perverts the spirit. Having, unlike Shaw, little concern for the dynamics of society, he could satisfy his aim of doing 'big work' only by expressing inner conflicts. The majority of O'Neill's works are top-heavy experiments, loaded with meaning borrowed piecemeal from Nietzsche Freud, Jung and Adler.

Chekhov worked in a national tradition which allowed him to realize in the drama what was best in himself. No matter how personal his art may be, it drew nourishment from the great stream of 19th century Russian realism. Russian writers shook off foreign classical and romantic influences and attempted to create a national literature. They became the ablest realists of Europe by a process as natural as breathing. Masters like Gogol, Turgenev, Tolstoy, Dostoyevsky, Chekhov and Gorky are second to none in the art of revealing life instead of sugarcoating it. From the beginning, their revelations were completely devoid of sensationalism. The well-spring of their art was humanness. Realism in Flaubert and Maupassant had a brain but realism in the Russian writers had a heart.

If Tolstoy by virtue of his heroic and moral spirit might have become modern Europe's Aeschylus, Chekhov was surely its Sophocles. In an oppressive world he retained a lovable simplicity and sweetness of temper. Both as a person and writer he possessed the ancient Sophoclean balance-without relinquishing an iota of truth about the realities that faced him without and clawed at him from within. 'Without' was the Russia of the old regime—the dispirited and listless pre-revolutionary intelligentsia, the ignorant and hardened peasantry and the barbaric penal system. 'Within' was the pained consciousness of these realities and the lack of progress in his country.

More than any other dramatists, Chekhov departs from the classic and romantic concepts of tragedy. Tragedy, he says in effect, is not the result of a clash between individuals but of attrition. What is most tragic about any ordinary life is that it is gradually worn away and impoverished. The will is atrophied, the nerves are tangled, the mind is befuddled and life simply wears thinner and thinner.

Chekhov achieves a poetry of emotions and environment which the greatest realists and naturalists have rarely failed to instil into their work. This poetry abounds in the best work of Ibsen, Synge and O'Neill. Chekhov creates it by means of a mood that consists of alternate shadings of despair and hope, tears and laughter.

In the German-speaking world, the most notable theatrical development came from Bertolt Brecht. He was not only a distinguished poet and playwright but an original stage director. Applying his 'epic theatre' philosophy, Brecht favoured detached artistry as against a theatre of complete illusion and empathy. According to Brecht, the stage should enlighten rather than induce emotional orgies. Special attention was paid in central Europe to his original and powerful chronicle of the thirty years' war in Germany, *Mother Courage.* Brecht wrote *Mother Courage* in exile at the beginning of the Second World War. Mr. Puntila and his servant Matti was a satirical extravaganza on the relations between master and man. His parables *The Caucasian Circle of Chalk* and *The Good Woman of Setzuan,* written while Brecht had been in exile in the United States, were especially worthnoting as examples of his theatrical and poetic talent. Brecht brought inventive dramaturgy and pungent dialogue, as well as vigorous lyrics, to the theatre.

John Gassner was able to confront the dreaded forties with the following conclusion to the original 1940 edition of *Masters of the Drama* :

> No finis can be written to the story of the drama, not even now that Europe is fighting its second great war since 1914. The theatre's search goes on, and its object is, as it has always been Man . . . . A great art has transcribed mankind's errors and aspirations for nearly three thousand years and has conveyed both its bestiality and divinity. This art has survived many

> catastrophes. It will no doubt survive the eminent ones of our times . . . . Over the entrance to every honourable theatre, whether it be devoted to laughter or suffering one might confidently engrave two ancient and indispensable words ! Nil Desperandum— Never Despair." Gassner's words proved true because the stage held its ground even during the dark interim of the war.[10]

It is against this backdrop of developments that Miller's drama may be explicated.

A deep sense of social consciousness is an intrinsic tenet of Arthur Miller's tragic stance, but beyond that his plays are universal tragedies. He makes the allegorical theatre creating 'the protagonist in search', his Everyman in whom he dramatizes the struggle of contemporary man with the forces of his age. Richard Chase rightly explains that the American novel from Hawthorne to Faulkner has individualised itself in a form distinguished from its European counterpart dealing with fables rather than stories, creating allegories rather than plots.[11] American drama shows the same contours: its significance lies in its allegorical pattern and not in its photo-phonographic transcription. O'Neill, Elmer Rice, Lawson, Barry, Thronton Wilder, T.S. Eliot, Arthur Miller, Tennessee Williams, William Inge and Edward Albee— each of them has pursued the allegorical theme of the twentieth century man journeying through the confusion of his time, wavering between despair and hope, drift and meaning. The quest motive like the phoenix, has been reborn in each case. O'Neill's *The Hairy Ape* came out to 'dig at the roots of the sickness of today'. The theme of expressionism presented in the format of journey and dealing with the futility of man's struggle in a world dominated by materialism and bureaucracy with Everyman as the hero has its parallels in Joyce's *Ulysses* and Eliot's *The Waste Land* but in American drama it finds a sustenance all through. Elmer Rice's *The Adding Machine,* Lawson's *Roger Bloomer,* Phillip Barry's *Hotel Universe,* Eliot's plays, Wilder's *Our Town and the Skin of Our Teeth* are variations upon the same allegorical journey pattern. Arthur Miller, like Tennessee Williams and Edward Albee, attempts to create an allegorical expressive form to his tragic vision. *All My Sons* explores man's obligation to assume responsibility. Death of a salesman deals with the tyranny of the American myth. *Incident at Vichy* deals with what Miller calls 'literal situation as well as the moral and ethical situation' (in which a group of people) are faced with the need to respond to total destruction. The theme of 'The Crucible' was the handing over conscience to another . . . and the realization that with conscience goes the person. In fact, a careful explication of Miller's dramatic tenor reveals the moral concern of the playwright. Like Williams, Miller is deeply concerned with the ethical function of theatre, like Ibsen, Strindberg, Chekhov, Tolstoy, Shaw and O'Neill, Miller has used the theatre as a platform for interpreting the human dilemma in the twentieth century as a crisis of conscience, as a growing conflict within human consciousness. For Miller as for Dante the essential purpose of the theatre is to show man the root of his suffering and its function to play out humanity's crisis to give its tortured consciousness a concrete shape. He was not a devout practising Jew, yet he acknowledges that he did absorb certain viewpoints, a commitment to the continuity of life and the need to go on even though there is a tragedy in the world.

This connects Miller to Morality plays of the 15th century and more directly to the modern European and continental drama. Artaud affirms that "a play is willy-nilly metaphysical and it is just its metaphysical bearing. I should say the intensity of its metaphysical efforts that comprises its essential worth."[12]

Ionesco also means the same when he says "since the artist apprehends reality directly, he is a true philosopher."[13] Gilman gives it a definite tone "it is in the union of dramatic imagination with philosophical intention that the triumph of the modern stage lies."[14] In truth, modern drama has become a kind of metaphysics that seeks to rediscover man, to bring him again in Artaud's words, "to his place between dream and events." Jean-Paul Sartre writes in his essay on the theatre in France that it is the responsibility of the drama to help modern man discern the ultimate significance of his own life. He further asserts that it is the specific function of the theatre to provide an appropriate structure for moral exploration, to create a form in which the human dilemma—in its present dimension may be given vivid expression.

With the emergence of the expressionist playwrights of the 1920's and the existentialist playwrights of the 1940's all the nice idealism of the old worlds completely disappeared. The Existentialist's dilemma of human life and the

Ahsurdist's perception of its littleness and insignificance whose seedlings were planted by the "sick hurry, divided aim and palsied heart" in Arnold's iron time of doubts destructions and fear, form part of the stacatto rhythm of life and literature in our time. The spirit of scientific rationalism with its wholesale attack on supernational belief caused an explosion of excessive liberty to the inquiring mind and opened up fresh avenues of exploration. "Each great discovery of the free mind, while it promised control over the accidents of nature and history, turned out, paradoxically, to show more obviously the isolation of man in time and nature."[15] Darwin's formula of evolution cut man adrift from his metaphysical origins and placed him on a chessboard of biology whereas Marx's investigations into the process of dialectical materialism revealed the human world to be no more than an economic game of the producer and the buyer. Freud's explorations showed the inner motivations, relegating man to the position of a helpless victim of unconscious drives, "an automation dancing to the tune called by internal forces."[16] The political history of Europe which is a record of upheavals, wars and conflicts shattered whatever illusions for a better future man might have and sundered all his hopes. As a consequence of all this, no sensitive writer worth the name should remain untouched by the panorama of colossal wastage and drift to general despair.

With Wagner and Ibsen, drama had identified itself with the rising critical spirit of the time. In the revolt of theatre that was launched with them and that still continues, a metaphysical dimension was added to drama. Eric Bentley and Robert Brustein have taken pains to pinpoint the modulations of this new spirit in drama. To many a writer, true poetry is another name for true drama. Artaud affirms that a play "is willy-willy metaphysical and it is just its metaphysical bearing, I should say the intensity of its metaphysical effort, that comprises its essential worth."[17] There is another variant of Ionesco's famous comment in which the distinction between art and philosophy is sought to be obliterated :

> Since the artist comprehends reality directly, he is a true philosopher. And it is the broadness, the depth, the sharpness of philosophical vision, his living philosophy which determine his greatness.[18]

Gilman echoes the views of Ionesco when he says that, "it is in the union of dramatic imagination with philosophical intention that the triumph of the modern stage lies."[19] What these critics hint at is that a philosophical drama is not merely an expression of a set of ideas but it is integral with a philosophical vision. Its chief aim is the formulation of a metaphysics that seeks to rediscover man, to bring him again, in Artaud's words, "to his place between dream and events."[20] The plays of Ibsen, Strindberg and Shaw achieve this aim to a large measure, reinterpreting and relocatng man in his own image.

However, it is fairly obvious that the modern critics' assessment of American drama is not quite fair or legitimate. For one thing these critics seem to lament over the lack of philosophical strain in modern American drama, for another, the American playwright is shown as being alien to his native tradition. As Brustein observes :

> In his subject matter, his writing style, his associations, his attitude and his ideas, the dramatist is far removed if not completely cut off from the mainstream of intellectual and literary discourse.[21]

According to Richard Gilman,

> The American drama is itself almost mindless; we weep for the intellectual deficiencies of Miller and Williams and for the existence of O'Neill as our monument to the hair-breadth victory of naked will and raw energy over language and idea, a victory that nonetheless leaves the major laurels on other brows.[22]

Both Gilman and Brustein seem to be the victims to the fallacy of their own logic. Admittedly, a good deal of thinking has gone into the making of drama, whether American continental or European. Philosophy is no longer the champagne of the select; it is the bread for each man's sustenance. It is good to locate this philosophical strain in the works of contemporary dramatists but wrong to say that modern American drama has no trace of it. Far from it, O'Neill, Miller and Williams are as deeply philosophical as any other major continental playwright. In fact, modern drama is distinct from the drama of earlier ages in that it is neither the expression of a particular culture, nor the gift of a particular nation. Its character is truly international. It is the consummate idiom of the new man who, stripped of all illusions, is trying to find himself.

O'Neill, Miller and Williams also belong to this international style of dramaturgy. This have much in common with the great dramatists all of all time—Ibsen, Brecht and Shaw, not to speak of Shakespeare. John Gassner rightly suggests that "a sense of extra theatrical purpose is as marked in the work of an effective anti-realist like Bertolt Brecht as in the work of a great realist Ibsen, and is as decisive in the comic genius of Bernard Shaw as in the tragic sense of O'Neill and Miller."[23]

A major concern of art in the twentieth century has been the questioning attitude toward the ideologies of the past. Various areas of thought attack, offer substitutes for, or strive for reconciliation with standards which in some cases have been accepted for almost two thousand years. Drama has been the most effective medium for the reenactment of this dilemma, which stations man between the past and a future that promises greater revolution than any previous change in Western culture.

> The result is the evolution of a type of drama more allegorical than any since the Middle ages. American drama's emergence into significance parallels in time the influence of allegorical drama from the European continent.[24]

American playwrights have produced plays which engage their hero in an action appropriately suited to the problems of all men in this period.

> The allegorical theme of twentieth century man journeying through the confusion of this period is the most unifying element to appear thus far in

> American drama, and it is this element which most closely identifies American drama with other forms of artistic expression in our time.[25]

American playwriting in its period of emergence after 1920 turned to the continent for its inspiration and its ideas: to the realism of Ibsen, the psychology of Strindberg, the psychiatry of Freud, the philosophy of Bergson and to that combination of elements called 'Expressionism' —a form of dramatic writing which originated with Strindberg and which received the utmost attention from the German play-wrights after 1910. To the fundamentals of naturalism already established, Strindberg gave a new method of presentation in such plays as *The Dance of Death* and *A Dream Play* and determinism through instinct and milieu received a new psychology. In these plays Strindberg abandoned the photography of realism, the dramatic sequence of events for a stream of consciousness in terms of stage symbols whereby the surface of life becomes disjointed, scattered, as in a dream to suggest the inner reality which lies beneath that surface. Not concerned with externals, the dramatists explores the idea, the source of conduct, until reality becomes subconsciousness and character mere abstraction. Scenes are often brief, they sometimes succeed one another without time sequence: they have neither order nor unity and they suggest, as they alternate between reality and fantasy, between objective action and analysis, the disorderly, disconnected features of a psychoanalysis.

The expressionistic technique introduced by Strindberg was destined to have far reaching influence upon the literature of the twentieth century expressionism-with other forms of twentieth century. It established for drama an alliance with symbolist movement in poetry, with the stream-of-consciousness novel, and with the impressionistic forms in music and painting.

In fact, most of the expressionistic playwrights started as realists. Strindberg wrote realistic plays before he embarked upon symbolist and expressionistic mode of writing. O'Neill began as a realist, wrote some of the best expressionist plays of the century and then went back to realism. Elmer Rice, Arthur Miller, Tennessee Williams, Thronton Wilder and a number of other playwrights did the same. Among the Americans playwrights only O'Neill, Miller and Williams could successfully fuse realism into their expressionistic technique.

Expressionism is not entirely a new art. One may find its origin in some of the plays of Shakespeare, in *Everyman* and in the Greek tragedies. The witches in Shakespeare's *Macbeth.* So, the wandering woman in Aeschylus's *Prometheus Bound,* characters like Good Deed, Fellowship in *Everyman* are forerunners of expressionistic characters. There was an attempt at expressionistic characterization even in the medieval plays. In these plays a simultaneous presentation of the hell, Paradise, the garden of Eden and the place where Christ died was made. Such a simultaneity gave a symbolic or allegorical meaning to the events presented. The sins and sufferings mentioned in the Bible were also reenacted in contemporary costumes and language.

Hauptmann, Kaiser, Toller and Capek added the theme of contemporary social and economic issues to the expressionist mode pioneered by Strindberg.

> No longer an individual, the protagonist becomes a member of a class, a collective hero engaged in the class struggle. The dramatic personae bear such names as Man, Woman, Millionaire, Doctor—classified as worker, slave or master and identified with abstractions like revolt, submission, justice, energy. The theme might be the eventual destruction to result from industrial and military developments as in Kaiser's *Gas Trilogy,* the inability of revolution to solve the mass problem, as in Toller's *Man and Masses,* or the danger of man's submission to the mastery of the machine as in Capek's 'AUR'.[26]

In creating a hero engaged in a struggle representative of a class, the expressionist playwright became the late descendant of the creator of the Morality play of the fifteenth century. Not concerned with the vices and virtues of the medieval religionist, the expressionist substitutes for them the dynamic concepts of contemporary civilization, brotherhood, economic equality, communism, fascism, democracy. For the devil, he substitutes materialism in one form or another, and for God, the life force or elan vital of Bergson. His hero, nevertheless, remains Everyman, even engaged in a contest for survival, the terms of which are the fundamental issues of the present age.

> The expressionist has allied himself with, or perhaps even fortified, the whole contemporary movement of

> allegory in art, expressed in terms of 'Journey' which originated long ago in the 'odyssey' and two civilisations later became the medieval morality play victimized in Everyman.[27]

Many of the plays of European expressionism were staged in New York in the early twenties, and the American playwrights turned to the form for inspiration. Influential though it was, expressionism remained an influence. No American playwright chose to write exclusively in this form. It was a form which lent itself to experimentation, and the playwright combined its elements with others. However, hardly an American playwright had not yielded to the influence to produce his own *Everyman* in which he dramatized from his point of view the struggle of contemporary man with the forces of his age. Arthur Miller made liberal use of the method and content of expressionism to write *Death of a Salesman.* Thronton Wilder culminated his journey into optimism with the allegorical *Our Town* and *The Skin of Our Teeth.* Archibald Macleish restated the conclusion to his poetic quest in a contemporary staging of the oldest search of all, Job's.

In a realistic theatre the emphasis was laid on physical realism. A drawing room with familiar furniture, commonsense dialogue and ordinary conversation formed parts of the play. But the expressionist drama is based on psychological realism. To the expressionist dramatist reality is something that man daily cheats himself into believing. To him realism is a mere illusion which preserves only the appearance of reality and not a revealing image of it, and therefore, he tries to throw some special light on reality on shifting his dramatic focus from the external to the interior. He creates various symbols and symbolic devices to project the inner world of the play on the stage.

So many of the old conventions have been used by the expressionist dramatist in different ways. A dramatist like O'Neill used masks most liberally. In his *Emperor Jones* and *The Great God Brown* the characters wear masks to reveal the private and the public masks that people wear in their lives. Arthur Miller used 'the flashback' in his *Death of a Salesman.* Willy Loman, the protagonist recalls to his mind the past events in his life and they are thus featured simultaneously on the stage. In most of the expressionist plays the set serves as an allegorical form for the substance of the play.

Henry Popkin in his critical essay, "Arthur Miller: The Strange Encounter" posits three of Miller's plays as parables or fables which explains why the characters can't be individuals.[28] Arthur Miller's regular practice in his plays is "to confront the dead level of banality with the heights and depths of guilt and to draw from this strange encounter a liberal parable of hidden evil and social responsibility. Each of his mature full-length plays (*All My Sons, Death of a Salesman, The Crucible and A View from the Bridge)* exhibits the same basic pattern, each one matches ordinary, uncomprehending people with extraordinary demands, and accusations. The characters are like the man in the old Jewish story who asks the price of bacon and then shudders at the sound of thunder out of the heavens; he protests meekly that he was only asking the price. Thunder sounds abruptly for Miller people too. From day to day they live their placid, apparently meaningless lives and suddenly the eternal intrudes thunder sounds the trumpet blows and these startled mediocrities are whisked off to the bar of justice."[29] In the midst of banality, guilt appears : "you killed twenty one fliers. You lived your life by false standards. You betrayed your wife and thereby caused her to be charged with witchcraft. You have condemned a family to starve. The little man protests: "What is the cosmos doing in my tacky living room? Must I decide the fate of the world ? Am I my brother's keeper ?" The crime is betrayal, the verdict is guilty and the sentence is death. Punishment is imposed, directly or indirectly, by the victim himself.

The families of *All My Sons* and *Death of a Salesman* do not belong to any discernible ethnic group. They are deliberately made the washed out, colourless representatives of society in general. Miller himself was apparently endeavouring to assert the non-sectarian universality of *Death of a Salesman.*

Keller and Loman are made as general as possible so that they may play the role of Everyman in their dramatic parable. Eddie Carbone of *A View from the Bridge,* is at least a cousin to Everyman, he is a Italo-American longshoreman and his ancestry is significantly Sicilian. The Greek associations of Sicily encourage Miller to call the play a tragedy and even so to employ a chorus. Also Eddie Carbone speaks verse of a sort. Miller retreated to prose when *A View from the Bridge* reappeared in the collected plays. But he had written in his preface to the earlier text: 'Verse reaches always toward the general statement. . . it is the most public of public speech.' He found a corresponding wideness of reference in the kind of play he was writing, 'social drama' a genre which he takes to include Greek tragedy : "To put it simply, even over-simply, a drama rises in stature and intensity in proportion to the weight of its application to all men." In this play, as in his other serious dramas, Miller had written a parable which was intended to apply to everyone. Joe Keller is every man facing a responsibility to his nation in war time. Willy Loman is every low man in our economic order. *The Crucible,* written at a time when many spoke of witch hunts directed against political heresy, was obviously designed to display a political parallel to our time in the salem witch trials. And *A View from the Bridge* is Greek, poetic and therefore all the more public in its object lesson on the folly of betrayal. The plays are dramatic parables or fables; their characters are as typical as the prodigal son or Aesop's lambs or wolves. They are as unattached and as non-sectarian as the medieval Everyman, and that is why they cannot be individuals."[30]

Richard Loughlin in his article entitled "Tradition and Tragedy in All My Sons" discovers Biblical parallels in theme and other respects, relating the play to characters in to Old Testament, the ancient Greek epics and medieval morality plays.[31]

Why did Arthur Miller entitle his play *All My Sons.* He might have called it, "the killer, A Season of Treason, what is cracking or even the false Prophet of Profit." What did he hope to accomplish by calling it *All My Sons?*

"Obviously, he is preaching 'brotherhood', using the Old Testament as both his text and his texture. The Book of Genesis (IV, 9) tells us about the first killer Cain. How did Cain respond to his Lord's inquiry concerning the whereabouts of Abel, his brother and his victim?" Am I my brother's keeper?

> What is Arthur Miller answer to Cain's counter question? Yes, you are your brother's keeper. You are responsible for the welfare of others. Selfishness is Painful; personal sacrifice is the only real test of love. To be successful means to be truthful. Honesty is real. Dishonesty is an illusion that disillusions. It is a shadow, the absence of true substance. Failure is not a matter of dollars and cents: failure means following false gods; the golden calf, the Almighty Dollar.[32]

We can listen Chris talking to Ann about his Army experience:

> It takes a little time to toss that obb. Because they weren't just men. For instance, one time it'd been raining several days and this kid came to me, and gave me his last pair of dry socks. Put them in my pocket.... but that's the kind of guys I had. They didn't die; they killed themselves for each other. I mean that exactly; a little more selfish and they'd've been here today. And I got an idea—watching them go down. Everything was being destroyed, see, but it seemed to me that one thing was made. A kind of ... responsibility. Man for man.... And then? I came home and it was incredible. I .... there was no meaning

> to it here; the whole thing to them was a kind of a bus accident. I went to work with Dad and that rat race again .... Because nobody was changed at all. It seemed to make anckers out of a lot of guys. I felt wrong to be alive to open the bank-book, the drive the new car, the see the new refrigerator. I mean you can take those things out of a man but when you drive that can you've got to know that it came out of the love a man can have for a man, you've got to be a little better because of that. Otherwise what you have is really loot, there's no blood on it. I didn't want to take any of it. And I guess that included you.[33]

In Miller's modern version and underscoring of the biblical story, Joe is Cain; Larry and the twenty-one P40 pilots who have lost their lives are Abel. Chris elicits from Joe the realization that all men are his sons and there are no missing links in the chain of humanity. In this respect, *All My Sons* is a morality play, because each of us is Everyman.[34]

As in Greek tragic epics, Chris avenges the suicide of his brother and the death of the p40 pilots. He cracks his father's defective code of life, his heart and his mind because the latter had cracked cylinder heads and his foreman's reputation.

A less self-righteous person might have salvaged Joe, a despicable man with a sluggish conscience but not completely hopeless. Short-sighted and selfish to a deplorable degree-unimaginative, unpatriotic, greedy, unprincipled, uncivilized and uncouth—Joe needed a rebirth—a reconstruction—not self-destruction. Chris, who says he loves his father, unfortunately had never read Maritain's definition of love, "the gift of self" or Shakespeare's sublime line "love does not alter when it alteration finds." If love does not teach Chris, charity could have. Compassion counsels us to hate the crime but to continue to love the criminal who is the slave of his error. Even bestial Joe Keller knew this much. In Act III, he tells his wife : "There's nothing he could do that I wouldn't forgive, because he's my son. Because I'm his father and he's my son .... Nothing bigger than that. And you're goin' to tell him, you understand? I'm his father and he's my son and if there is something bigger than that I'll put a bullet in my head!"

We may recollect how the great Teacher, coming upon the people preparing to stone the harlot, Mary Magdalene, said : "Let him who is without sin cast the first stone". "She was salvaged by unselfish love, just as Joe could have been. Again, according to Richard L. Loughlin :

> The originality of Michaelangelo and Shakespeare began with the digging up of old vases and manuscripts .... For some strange reason man must always thus plant his fruit trees in a graveyard. Man can only find life among the dead. In *All My Sons* Arthur Miller found life among the "dead"—the characters in the Old Testament, the ancient Greek epics and the medieval morality plays such as

> *Everyman.* He has protected us from the provincialism of the present by echoing some of the literary and spiritual traditions of Western culture.[35]

Where ethnic association may be vague, the characters' occupations in Miller's plays are loaded with symbolic usefulness. Joe Keller must be engaged in war work and it must be possible for his son in the air force to make use of the products he manufactures: the son's suicide is a public acknowledgement of guilt. There can be no more suitable emblem of our commercial society than the salesman Willy Loman, especially since we are never told what he sells. In a sense he sells himself, but the product wears out.

These plays argue cases: they prove points. Each play is constructed to expose a pattern of guilt, to find out who is guilty and to impose the penalty of death. The plot drives us from one to another of the devastating points which the prosecutor-dramatist makes against his characters. The purpose of *All My Sons* was, according to Miller, "to bring a man into the direct path of the consequences he had wrought." Up to the time of the play's action Joe Keller has avoided consequences by avoiding the discovery of his guilt. By the end of the second act, his guilt is established, with the help of a clue that any respectable mystery would be ashamed to use. Keller had pretended illness on the day his company approved some cracked cylinder heads for the Air Force. He gives himself away by inadvertently referring to his unfailing good health. The case is nearly complete, but Keller still refuses to take personal responsibility. In the last act, his son produces a letter— what is so telling as documentary evidence ? In which another son reveals that he committed suicide because of his father's misdeeds. Keller quits arguing and shoots himself just in time to prevent his son from turning him over to the authorities.

In fact, Miller's goal is to demonstrate an idea. The idea in *All My Sons* is the most elementary conception of social responsibility, as for the characters. Miller has informed us that he knows "how rarely the great issues penetrate such environments. "Two simplicities collide—the idea and the man and we recognize that on this dramatic railroad, Miller has constructed only one track.

Death of a Salesmen is also to a great degree constructed as an investigation. Willy Loman hunts the secret of his failure, he wants to know the right path. His mistake is that there is no right path; there is, however, a wrong path and Willy has travelled on it for most of his life. He asks his brother Ben and his neighbour Charley for the secret, they cannot tell him, and he cannot guess that it does not exist. He stumbles upon telltale clues and significant discoveries, but he manages to ignore most of them. It is his son Biff who plays detective more successfully. Present events make Biff see his lies about the past he perceives the hollowness of the dream of success from the start. The real hostage of success Willy Loman remains unaltered. But once more, the terms of the courtroom apply to this play. Willy's offences against his sons, against society are exposed so that sentence can be passed. Miller describes Willy as a man who "has broken a law" in which he deeply believes.

The Crucible, too, turns upon a law which we should not respect : "Thou shall not permit a witch to live." It takes the form of an investigation, for it begins with the arrival of the great investigator of witches. Our pursuit of the facts takes us over two paths; while the witch hunters make their efforts to measure the extent of witchcraft in the community. We follow John Proctor's attempt to weigh the guilt peters out since his guilt is nothing beside the community's. The issues are made a good deal simpler than those of the earlier plays. In our eyes, the community condemns itself, totally and without qualification, as it builds its airtight case against John Proctor. Contrasting his crime with the court's the defendant justifiably thinks better of himself : "Now I do think I see some shred of goodness in John Proctor."

A View from the Bridge also has at its core the proving of a case. Eddie Carbone desperately endeavours to conceal from himself and from the world his incestuous passion for his niece. He bitterly resents Rodolpho, the young man he favours, but he feels obliged to make his hatred publicly acceptable by providing Rodolpho to be a homosexual. He seizes Rodolpho and kisses him, then goes to a lawyer to offer this incident as proof that "the guy ain't right." Ultimately, Eddie uses the assumption of homosexuality and opportunism to justify him in turning Rodolpho and his brother into the immigration authorities. To his death, he continues to plead his case, protesting the pure motives behind his treacherous action. But, obviously, we must conclude that informers, like the accusors of witches, must be themselves be brought to judgement and that a verdict must returned against them. Miller is more compassionate toward this informer, who is proved to be merely sick and not like Abigail in *The Crucible* totally deprived.

Each of Miller's protagonists fights for his good name, for the respect of his community, for a public verdict the idea that he owes anything to society, he is won over by his sons. One has killed himself because he joins in the public condemnation which his father has ignored. The other son lives by his star, "the star of one's honesty"—a fitting symbol for the character the world attributes to him. Joe recognizes, as his sons have done that he cannot live for his family alone that he and his family belong to the world and therefore he commits suicide because he cannot live without his good name.

Willy Loman also plays to an audience: he is a Salesman who must require to be approved, to be well liked. As the drama progresses Willy's faltering claim on the respect and affection of others is matched by his new role as a horrible example, a public instance of the man for whom society has no further use.

John Proctor and Eddie Carbone die for their good name and makes no bones about it. Proctor refuses to put his name to the lies he has told to save his life. He will lie privately, but he will die rather than compromise his public integrity. "How may I live without my name ? I have given you my soul; leave me my name ? In a much worse cause, name from the man he has ruined; I want my name !.... Marco's got my name and you can run and tell him, kid, that he's gonna give it back to me in front of this neighbourhood, or we have it out." These are no private dramas; each frustrated, ruined hero compels attention, demands that some meaning be found in his catastrophe. Rightly or wrongly, he wants respect for his good name, even in defeat.

The line between good and eivil, between the good society and the oppressors, is always clearly drawn in Miller's plays. Biff Loman may not perceive the distinction soon enough and Willy Loman may never see it, but we are never permitted any doubts. Miller's bold certainty is best illustrated by his comments on *The Crucible*. Charged with making his witch-hunters too wicked. Miller replied that he did not make them wicked enough. "I believe now, as I did not conceive then, that there are people dedicated to evil in the world .... Evil is not a mistake but a fact in itself." Like the youngman is Shaw's *Major Barbara*. Miller is sure he knows "the difference between right and wrong", and he permits his heroes—Chris Keller, Biff Loman and John Proctor—to stand at last four square for righteousness. There could be no clearer demonstration of Miller's insistence that a play is a parable of right and wrong, a parable in which no blurring of distinctions is permitted.

America's outstanding writers of dramatic allegory—O'Neill, Eliot and Wilder have at mid century completed their cycle of thought. O'Neill confined the evolution of his to the drama. Eliot and Wilder chose the drama to climax a pattern of thinking begun and developed through other literary forms.

Both Tennessee Williams and Arthur Miller, like O'Neill before them in *The Hairy Ape,* came forth in the beginning of their careers with an allegorical commentary on man's maladjustment in modern world. Both are in the tradition of despair which originates in the plays of O'Neill, but other influences have played their part also. Williams and Miller returned to influences from the twenties apart from O'Neill's and Williams', at least, inherited elements which detour from O'Neill's descent into hell for an approach less prophetic of total doom.

If Williams represents a compromise with the world as Waste Land, he takes his place with other writers who have similarly effected such a compromise particularly Ernest Hemingway in the novel and Robert E. Sherwood in drama. *The Petrified Forest* appeared in 1935, one year after O'Neill declared embrace of spirituality in *Days Without End.* Eliot's conversion had already begun with *Ash Wednesday* in 1930, but Prufrock's regeneration would not be forthcoming for another ten years. For many in this decade, the effects of the depression and the continued influence of a world like Spengler's *Decline of the West* intensified the compulsion to despair set by the early Eliot and the early O'Neill. For some, Sherwood among them, the content of realism yielded to a romantic conclusion.

The Petrified Forest is simultaneously a melodrama and allegory. Borrowing from both forms, he managed to satisfy each contingent in his audience, those who would be entertained and those who would demand an association beyond the immediate one of cops and robbers on a lonely desert.

No setting could suggest more effectively a Waste Land than that used by Sherwood for this play. Sterility finds its theme in the barren, rocky acres of eastern Arizons where the land is only half desert, not yet given to the cremated, purifying sand but suggestive instead of a civilization in its best moments before death. Had Eliot become a playwright earlier, to translate his Waste Land into contemporary terms for the stage, he could not have chosen a setting more appropriate.

Williams' most important contemporary in the Post-War period is Arthur Miller. When Williams chose to interpret his world for the stage he was already an established play-wright with two great successes in *The Glass Menagerie* and *A Street Car Named Desire.* In *Death of a Salesman.* Miller wrote his first distinguished work, the tragedy of a man named Willy Loman, in whose conflict the author managed to transcend individual tragedy to include us all in his summation of what is wrong with our world. In his case, his allegory proved to be, thus far at least his best work, since neither of its successors *The Crucible* and *A View From the Bridge* is comparable in quality.

One aspect of American drama in the last decade is that it begins to subscribe to its own influences. Firmly established now, with names like O'Neill, Anderson, Eliot and Wilder on its roll, American drama can now function within its own traditions, no longer dependent entirely upon, European models. If in its staging *Camino Real* recalls an earlier effort of the twenties, so does Death of a Salesman in its recreation of the theme and method from *The Adding Machine* of Elmer Rice. The modified expressionistic method of scene presentation devised by Miller bears close resemblance to that of Rice and the theme of a small-town Salesman trapped in a capitalistic materialistic system echoes sharply the earlier presentation of an accountant frustrated by the same system. Miller's achievement seems now the more mature, since he treats with greater compassion and dignity man's predicament and achieves a denouncement which Rice yields as much to satire as to pathos. Both men have pursued the tragedy of the little man. But in dividing the blame for his predicament between man and society, as Rice did not do, Miller has not failed to observe that part of man's tragedy is to be little.

Death of a Salesman relates the story of an unsuccessful travelling Salesmen whose unfortunate values may be attributed both to social causes and to personal inadequacy, a man who must maintain at any price an ideal image of himself, since he never sees himself as he really is. Willy Loman emerges as a more complex figure than Mr. Zero, eliciting greater sympathy. Since he is never a protagonist but always a victim, a well-meaning, basically good, but helpless because his dreams are too big for him, his world too vicious, ready always to engulf him with the very standards he considers ideals.

In Miller, as in Sherwood, man's noblest act is to die, if by so doing he can compensate for his failure to achieve his dream. Unlike Sherwood, Miller portrays modern life in a realistic complexity which does not yield to heroics. Whereas Sherwood romanticizes, Miller apologizes— "He's not the finest character that ever lived. But he's a human being .... He had the wrong dreams .... He never knew who he was." Member of a commercial class which stands ready to cast him a side when he is no longer useful. Willy Loman does not possess either the potential to succeed by its standards or to recognize his failure.

If Arthur Miller's conclusion of despair offers any of compromise, it lies in his division of the blame between man himself and society. The rules imposed by society are not altogether the product of men in their time; they are the result of an evolutionary process begun before their period. Willy Loman subscribes to the ideals of his period. At the same time he has neither the skill to win through them or the realization necessary to cast them aside in view of their having failed him. This is an attitude which Miller acquired, no doubt, from O'Neill. It is one, too, which contributes most effectively to his interest in the tragedy of the 'little man'. Since *Death of a Saleman,* Miller has not evolved except as an experimental playwright. The theme of man going down to defeat in a materialistic society he abandoned first, for a theme of contemporary political freedom disguised as early American in *The Crucible* and afterward for a Freudian treatment of a little guy's downfall in *A View From the Bridge.* In a Preface to the last, he explained his interest in pursuing the tragic complexities of the average man, not in terms of contemporary values but in terms of those qualities in man which make him universally tragic. In view of such a statement, *Death of a Salesman* can be taken to represent his estimate of a man in his relationship to contemporary society.

The two most significant American dramatists to appear in the post-war period, Miller and Williams offer in their attitude an affinity perhaps not at once discernible in characterizations so different as Willy Loman and Kilroy. Both writers feel the need to apologize for everyman in a manner heretofore unknown. To both characters goes a profound degree of sympathy to Loman because he had the wrong dreams because he never knew who he was to Kilroy, despite his mistakes, because he had a heart of pure gold. Incapable of maturity both of them are but possessing an inherent goodness, nevertheless, a child-like innocence to which O'Neill never gave voice because he was either too Freudian or too bitter. But what draws these two writers even closer is a mutual neglect of God. He who has been of such grave concern to O'Neill, Eliot and Wilder receives from them not a mention. The street cleaners come for Kilroy because he has forsaken adventure and love. Loman drives himself to them with his failure to realize commercial success God, as either refuge or justification, receives no consideration from either of them.

Their neglect of Him would not go unchallenged. In 1958 another poet-turned-playwright recreated in a contemporary setting the story of Job and called his play. J.B. Almost from the beginning of his career as poet, Archibald Macleish has been in both poetic expression and philosophical explication T.S. Eliot's most successful associate. If Eliot has not thus far influenced any major American playwright, he has at least a follower who in turning to drama to echo the voices of his poetry, parallels even further Eliot's own career.

Macleish arrived at a dramatic form by way of one act plays and verse plays for radio. J.B. is closer to the conventional morality play than any other American allegory in play form. A poetic dialogue in play form it might be called from which emerges a characterization only vaguely contemporary. The effort to produce a protagonist universal in time and place has resulted in an almost complete absence of characterization, an absence which alongwith a resolution of action that is obvious and unexciting. Adding markedly to the revival of interest in expressionism in the fifties, Macleish makes use of such expressionistic devices as the discontinuity of scene, abstract rather than detailed characterization, multiple staging, the use of light to create atmosphere and even the use of masks.

Job as the inspiration for a modern morality is not new to American drama. Whether or not J.B. becomes 'one of the lasting achievements of art and mind in our time', it had its precedent in Phillip Barry's *Here Come the Clowns,* which was a much more itemized photograph of a modern counterpart of Job. Barry's play is precedential in setting also, for Macleish has chosen a scene not far removed from Barry's. The back-stage restaurant has become a circus tent, and the stage hands and vandvillains have been replaced circus vendors and actors. All the world's a stage, but the stage on stage is not infrequent locale for today's Journeying Everyman.

According to Louis Broussard, "As contemporaneous Everyman became a meaningful symbol in the novel and the poetry of the Post-War period, and Ulysses and Prufrock became the foremost representatives of a new literary movement, continental drama developed its own allegorical format known as expressionism.[36] American drama after 1920 subscribed to the influence of expressionism and obtained from it what was to remain the most distinctively unifying theme among the plays written during the forty years of its evolution. Eugene O'Neill and Elmer Rice were the first American writers of allegorical drama influenced by expressionism. In a single yet highly significant and influential play, *The Adding Machine* Elmer Rice examined in economic and spiritual terms the plight of the average man following the first world war and with an attitude at first sympathetic and then satiric reached a conclusion of helplessness. Eugene O'Neill was much longer and far more thorough in his analysis, which began with a dismissal of all ideas and institutions in *The Hairy Ape* and which continued for twenty-five years to waver between hope and despair until he gave hope its final rejection in *The Iceman Cometh,* a rejection which he reiterated in his three posthumous plays.

First to accept O'Neill's pessimism was Robert E. Sherwood who in *The Petrified Forest* faced squarely the issue that the ideas of man can no longer serve him, though he affirmed the possibility of regeneration through a new set of regeneration through a new set of ideals. Man in this age, they both agreed, is doomed.

Contradicting their negativism, Phillip Barry probed the psychological and religious aspects of modern man's dilemma and concluded that man can, first of all, subscribe to his own experience and profit therefrom and what he cannot resolve he should like Job accept as God's will. *Hotel Universe* and *Here Come the Clowns* anticipated the plays of T.S. Eliot, who alongwith Thronton Wilder undertook to continue the optimism inaugurated by Barry. Eliot repeated in plays like *The Cocktail Party* the spiritual conclusion of his later poems and Wilder extended to *Our Town* and *The Skin of Our Teeth* an abiding faith in the beauty and goodness of life.

Between 1949 and 1958 Arthur Miller, Tennessee Williams and Archibald Macleish produced allegorical plays with expressionistic stage craft not seen since the twenties. Accepting a tradition bequeathed him by Elmer Rice, Miller in *Death of a Salesman* presented a compassionate treatment of man in a similar predicament concluding in defeat. In *Camino Real* Williams chose the compromise first assumed by Robert E. Sherwood that the resurgence of hope sustains man while he continued in error and dies. In J.B. Macleish like Barry accepted the conclusion reached by Job so long ago.

As Louis Broussard would have it, "The American dramatist writes in a tradition of despair and negation which began when Ibsen and Chekhov first questioned reality and which gained impetus when Strindberg resolved their questions with attitude of futility and the expressionists took up the cry."[37] With the exception of Barry, whose attitude perhaps took root in his work in comedy, the American dramatists who have come to drama from other literary forms. Eliot and Macleish were poets who climbed the same winding stair to a spiritual decision and Wilder had already expressed his faith in life itself in several novels. At the end of the first half century of American drama, the faith of Eliot and Wilder has not yet overtaken the despairing conclusions of O'Neill, Sherwood, Williams and Miller, career dramatists who abide by a tradition introduced earlier on the continent.

According to Dr. N.S. Pradhan, "in Arthur Miller's plays; the quest becomes a search for identity, which coupled with a sense of guilt results in the recognition that the dream of perfection is hopeless."[38]

The Misfits, a short story that later became a screenplay, shows the holpelessness of the dream in the significant metaphor of the misfit. The three cowboys, although they are running from unfortunate past are rootless because of their contempt for steady and settled life. The irony of three outcasts is that whereas open spaces become their ideals of freedom, they trap, wild horses from these open spaces to sell them for food. Their exertion to bring about the 'Fall' of the stallion symbolizes the force of society to bring them (the Cowboys) to their knees. They do to the horses what society does to them. Because the horses represent what cow-boys seek, their aggressiveness turns back on themselves so that their dream of freedom becomes self-destructive. The last scene of the wild horses leaping in the air and "striking at the sky" in their captivity, underlines the paradox of the cowboys' lives. That is, their defiance of, and their dependence on society. But the dream of freedom will continue in exploring other regions till the wild horses are taken. Then perhaps, the dream will die or be transferred to another hopeless quest.

The strongest emphasis on the pursuit of dreams is in *Death of a Salesman* which is a play about dreams. Even the sets have a dream-like quality. The dream as a quest for paradise is embodied in Willy Loman who dreams two versions of the American dream : "the business-urban success dream" in which Miller sees himself as a successful tycoon and the rural agrarian dream which brings forth Willy's romantic escapist notions of a life of communion with nature. For the success dream, Willy's models are Dave Singleton (the perfect ex-salesman), Charley (the friendly neighbour) and Uncle Ben. Uncle Ben, following the Horatio Alger formula, had suddenly become rich. Even Howard (Willy's boss), whom the singleminded pursuit of 'success' has turned into a monster, is Willy's ideal. One cause of Willy's remorse is that he is a failure in the pursuit of this substitute of a dream—a failure in his own, as well as his family's eyes.

Willy's rural agrarian dream is a sort of safety valve to withdraw from the harsh realities of failure in the pursuit of success dream. This second dream is something to fall back upon in moments of great self-commiseration. It is indicated by the melody of grass and trees and horizon, and by Willy's vision of a hammock between two elmtrees. The symbolic scene in which Willy, facing final failure begins to plant a garden at night in the shadaw of the skyscraper is noteworthy. The end shows that both of Willy's dreams personify the tension between despair and hope that is inherent in the quest for Eden. Taken individually, the two dreams are equally hopeless as far as Willy is concerned. They provide meaning in his life because he can balance one dream against the other. Miller sees in Willy the struggle to pursue both the dreams at the same time. And his failure in one (success' dream) leads to his failure in the other. It is difficult to agree with the view that Miller's play is confused because of his failure to commit himself clearly to one of the two dreams of American culture embodied in Willy Loman. Miller as an artist is dealing with the tragic consequences of failure and guilt, rather than making a statement of sociological import.

References

1. John Gassner, *Masters of the Drama,* Dover Publications, INC, New York, p. 317.
2. *Ibid.*, p. 317.
3. *Ibid.*
4. *Ibid.,* p. 317.
5. W.B. Yeats : *The Second Coming,* 11. 3-4.
6. Robert Brustein : *The Theatre of Revolt,* Little Brown & Co., Boston, 1964, p.7.
7. Robert Brustein : *The Theatre of Revolt,* Little Brown & Co., Boston, 1964, pp. 23-24.
8. Bamber Cascoigne : *Twentieth Century Drama,* Hutchinson University Library, London, p. 17.
9. John Gassner : *Masters of the Drama,* Dover Publications, Inc, New York, 1954, p. 394.
10. John Gassner : *Masters of the Drama,* Dover Publications, Inc, New York, 1940, p. 692.
11. Richard Chase : *Quest for Myth,* Baton Rough, Louisiana State University Press, 1949, p. 24.
12. Quoted by Gilman in "The Drama is Coming Now", *The Modern American Theatre,* ed. Alvin B. Kernan, New Jersey, 1967, p. 31.
13. *Ibid.,* p. 31.
14. *Ibid.,* p.166.
15. Alvin B. Kernan : "A Discussion of the Modern Theatre", *The Modern American Theatre,* ed. Kernan, New Jersey, 1967, p. 29.
16. *Ibid.,* p. 29.
17. Quoted by Gilman : "The Drama is Coming Now", *The Modern American Theatre,* p.165.
18. *Ibid.*
19. *Ibid.*
20. *Ibid.,* p. 165.
21. Robert Brustein : "Why American Plays are not Literature", *American Drama Its Critics,* ed. A.S. Downer, Chicago and London, 1965, p. 249.
22. Richard Gilman : "The Drama is Coming Now", p. 31.
23. John Gassner : *Theatre at the Crossroads,* New York, 1960, p. 10.

24. Louis Broussard : *American Drama-Contemporary Allegory from O'Neill to Williams,* Norman, University of Oklahoma Press, 1966, p. 4.
25. *Ibid.,* p. 4.
26. Louis Broussard : *American Drama, Contemporary Allegory from O'Neill to Williams Norman,* University of Oklahoma Press, 1966, p. 5.
27. *Ibid.,* p. 6.
28. Henry Popkin : *Arthur Miller : The Strange Encounter, American Drama and its Critics,* Ed. Alan S. Downer, Chicago, 1965, p. 218.
29. *Ibid.,* p. 219.
30. *Ibid.,* p. 220.
31. Richard L. Loughlin : "Tradition and Tragedy in All My Sons: *English Record,* 14 No. 3, 1964, pp. 23-27.
32. *Ibid.,* p. 23.
33. Arthur Miller : *All My Sons,* Act I, Dell, Six Great Modern Plays, pp. 386-87.
34. Richard L. Loughlin : "Tradition and Traged in All My Sons". *English Record 14,* No. 3, 1964, p. 24.
35. *Ibid.,* p. 26.
36. Louis Broussard : *American Drama Contemporary Allegory from Eugene O'Neill to Tennessee Williams, Norman,* University of Oklahoma Press, 1986, p. 128.
37. *Ibid.,* p. 130.
38. N.S. Pradhan : *Modern American Drama,* Arnold Heinemann. New Delhi, 1978, p. 34.

2

The Island and The Continent

(All My Sons)

Chris	:	You can be better! Once and for all you can know there's a universe of people outside and you're responsible to it and unless you know that, you threw away your son because that's why he died. or
Keller, Pleading	:	Chris, a man cann't be a Jesus in this world!

Arthur Miller made his professional appearance as a full-fledged playwright with *The Man Who Had All the Luck.* The play was produced on Broadway on Nov. 23, 1944 and lasted for four performances. The play gives the impression of being the work of a beginner, a novice in the art of playwriting. It seems contrived, but not well contrived. The crucial situation at the end of the last act is strong, but artificial, a theatrically constructed situation rather than a real and inevitable one. The characters are clearly drawn but some are purely illustrative and are dropped when their purpose is served, rather than being meaningfully interwoven throughout the story. All the characters seem fugitives from a regional folk-drama and this tendency is especially noticeable in the first act. The point may be clear just by listing some of their names—J.B. Feller, Amos Beeves, Hestar Falk, Den Dibble.

The main quality of the play is its stress on moral responsibility. The cardinal character, David Frieber, or David Beeves as he was called in the production version, feels guilty for having been successful without real merit or effort. He feels destined to pay for his good luck by the stillbirth of his child. If his child's death makes up for his unmerited good luck, he can then, he feels, sink all of his efforts into raising mink and can succeed for once by his own abilities. When the child is born perfectly healthy. David becomes observed by his need for his success until his wife forces him to let the mink die although the death of the animals will wipe away most of their prosperity.

A sub-plot in the play concerns Patterson Beeves, whose life and energy have been devoted to the dream of turning his son Amos into a champion baseball players. David kindly arranges for a talent scout to watch Amos in action and one of the most moving scenes in the play is when the scout turns him down.

The relationship between Amos and Pat Beeves in this play is an embryonic form of the father-son antagonism that was to occupy the two later plays. *All My Sons* and *Death of a Salesman*. In all three works, a well-meaning father forfeits the respect of his son by forcing him to accept his own standard of success. Pat Beeves tries to mould Amos into a baseball pitcher. On the whole the play reads like a moral. fable dealing with the themes of money, morality and father-son relationship.

In *The Man Who Had All the Luck,* Arthur Miller tries to probe exact part that fate plays in the life of man. Despite all good luck, Beeves is causing to "accumulate around his own head an invisible but palpable fund, so to speak, of retribution." As people are frustrated in one way or other, he thinks he, too, will be frustrated. He waits for some, disaster to strike him but nothing happens. His friends fail simply through 'bad luck'. The idea of an unseen fate guiding human destiny drives him mad but he is happy the moment he thinks that his own ability and careful action are responsible for his success.

Speaking of the flaws of the play, Dennis Welland observes:

> A dramatization of luck is likely to strain coincidence to breaking to point and by the end of the opening scene when Hester's father has been killed pushing the car, he is too mean-minded to allow David to overhaul—and killed by the very vehicle on the repair of which David's lucky career is to be based. But those who are prepared to accept this amount of luck may well be deterred by the monkey-tricks of the next scene where the arm is extended further to pull more chestnuts out. The orphan David has been given until the following morning to repair the Marmon : he is little of a mechanic and in any case the theme requires him to succeed by luck, not by ability .... Despite the fairytale element, this play is far more of a hang over from the 1930's than

> either *All My Sons* or *Death of a Salesman* which have been less justly attacked on that score.[1]

Miller's adaptation of Ibsen's *An Enemy of the People* was produced on Broadway on December 28, 1950. But despite a cast headed by Fredric March, Florence Eldridge and Morris Carnovsky, it lasted only 36 performances. Although not an eloquent play, Miller's version is fluent and streamlined, colloquial and easy. Many of Ibsen's long expositions and tirades are drastically reduced, so that the adaptation is only about two-thirds the length of the original.

Miller wrote this adaptation with moral earnestness and a greater sense of social responsibility. Miller himself admits "the central theme of *An Enemy of the People,* is in my opinion, the central theme of our social life today."[2] He further finds it an enduring theme, in fact, possibly the most enduring of all Ibsen's themes—because there never was nor will there ever be, an organised society able to countenance calmly—the individual who insists that he is right while the vast majority is absolutely wrong."[3] The reason for Miller's adapting this particular play becomes obvious by these statements. For Miller it is simply the question of whether one's vision of truth ought to be a source of guilt at a time when the mass of man condemn it as a dangerous and devilish lie. The same view impelled the working of the 'Crucible' and the same problem Miller had to face six years later when he was called to appear before the House Committee on un-American activities. *An Enemy of the People* suggests the answer that when the times are out of joint; the individual must be true to himself. Stockman clings to the truth and suffers the social consequence. The play is concerned with the inviolability of objective truth. The people who attempted to warp the truth for ulterior purposes must inevitably become warped and corrupted themselves. The play is the story of a scientist who discovers an evil and innocently believes that he has done a service to humanity. He expects that he will be thanked by the people. However, the town has a vested interest in the perpetuation of that evil and his 'truth', when confronted with that interest, must be made to conform. The scientist cannot change the truth for any reason disconnected with the evil and this brings suffering for him. This theme is valid today just as it will always be in Miller's view.

For Miller the stage is the place for ideas, for philosophies and for the most intense discussion of man's fate. For him, Ibsen is one of the masters of discussion and that is why Miller gets influenced by him. Though Miller's *An Enemy of the People* does not appear as "an eloquent play"[4] as Robert Hogan finds it, it seemed extraordinarily contemporary in its concerns. *An Enemy of the People* went right to the heart of the question of an individual's will and ability to challenge the assumptions of his own society. Indeed, one of the play's characters precisely raises the question "without power, what good is the truth". Again he dramatises the plight of a man who must decide whether his responsibility is owed first to his family or to the wider world; whether the truth, indeed, is an absolute necessity.

Though not a powerful play, *The Man Who Had All The Luck* yet provided the basis and background on which Miller erected better and more purposeful plays. Miller himself said about this play that "far from being a waste and failure this play was a preparation and possibly a necessary one, for those that followed." Moreover, it is linked to *All My Sons* in many ways. Both the plays originated in real-life anecdotes Miller had heard; both have a mid-western setting and atmosphere.

All My Sons is the story of Joe Keller, a small manufacturer, who during the war allowed some faulty engines to be shipped to the air force. When a number of planes crashed, Keller and his partner were brought to trial. Keller was finally released and his partner blamed, although Keller himself was really responsible. The theme, then, is one of morality and money and the action centres around the attempt of Keller's son Chris to find the truth and to fix the responsibility and of Keller to avoid his responsibility. The point of his guilt is only brought home to his after a letter is produced proving that his other son Larry had also considered his father guilty and had died in combat as a kind of expiation. Then Joe recognizes that the other pilots who died were "All My Sons" and in expiation he kills himself.

This action does not at first dominate the play. It is brought to a head by the current action, a false plot which seems at the beginning to be the story's major substance. Chris has asked his brother's fiancee home because he intends to marry her. However, Chris' mother refuses to believe that Larry really died in battle and much of the play's first two acts is an attempt to convince her, so that Chris and Ann may marry.

As in *Oedipus Rex* or *Ghosts*, the real plot emerges from the present action like a ghost from the past. It comes to dominate that action and to be the centre of the play. This plot from the past even in the beginning of the play, is constantly intended. We are constantly reminded of Joe's trial and Larry's death. Such a technique may seem at first to slow the pace, until we see that it is revealing the real action. When such a parallel plot is well handled, there is suspenseful tension as the relationship between past and present becomes ever clearer.

Like Ibsen's social plays, Miller's play is economical. All of his characters, even the minor ones, have an integral relation to the theme. No characters are introduced merely to illustrate or to facilitate the mechanics of the plot. Such economy emphasizes the play's closeness to traditional austere tragedy. This is a family tragedy; the father is a man of some importance who falls from power to ignominy. The lives of his entire family are blighted by his crime. There is even in the play a hint of fate inexorably guiding the destinies of the characters. It is the ghost from the past, the dead son, whose words precipitate a tragic climax. In one of the minor characters who is preparing a horoscope of the dead son, the play even has a prophet. That last fact suggests the distance between the austere stylized tragedy of Sophocles and Racine and the austere realistic tragedy of Ibsen and Miller.

All My Sons is, according to Miller, a play written for a prophetic theatre. By a prophetic theatre he implied something "seriously meant for people of common sense, and relevant to both their domestic lives and their daily work and an experience which widens their awareness of connection ... the filaments to the past and the future which lie concealed in life."[5] Joe Keller makes profit by selling defective engines to the Air Force directly causing their pilots' deaths. He allows his subordinate Deever to be imprisoned and disgraced for his own crime. His own son, Chris Keller, the returned army officer, rejects his father. Joe Keller now realises that all those dead pilots were *All My Sons* and commits suicide. How greed and self-interest in business can circumvent one's social responsibility is illustrated in the play.

The advance on *The Man Who Had All The Luck* is evident both in theme and technique. The story is clearly a more important one — an aircraft engine-manufacturer with no conscience who supplies faulty cylinder heads in war time is likely to command more attention to and to raise wider issues than a mink farming mechanic with a conscience at once too sensitive and too narrow. Nevertheless, it is primarily at the domestic level that the problem is explored. The real value of the war framework lies in its topicality, in the audience - indignation that is universally generated against Joe Keller and in the social tensions and guilt that is set up in his sons. But there is never any question of these emotions promoting Chris to any form of political action or public protest — a point too obvious to need making, except that references to the play too often suggest that it is politically - directed. What concerns Miller here, as in most of his plays, is the impinging of the public issue on the private conscience and the domestic circle of the family. His achievement here, to put it at its lowest, lies in the verisimilitude with which he creates not only a convincing, homely family, but also the sense of the flow of communal life in a suburban neighbourhood. There is a suggestion of social density communicated here more skilfully and less obtrusively than in the earlier play : the Kellers are part of a town in a way that Frievers never were.

As with most of Miller's characters, there is no vice in Joe, only littleness and his own form of myopia. He is genuinely unable to visualise the public consequences of what was for him a private act. To have stopped production when the flaw was discovered would have endangered the future of the business that meant security to his family: it was as simple as that. Keller is no villainous capitalist egged on by competitive mania in a cut-throat world of business, nor is he the cynical profiteer deliberately reducing the margin of profit. Other dramatists would have seen him in this light and written the play that way. Miller sees him as the simple man who has got on the energy and will-power but who is hardly clever enough to know how he has done it. To this all the luck and there is more than a grain of truth in his wife's comment: "We're dumb, Chris. Dad and Jare stupid people. We don't know anything. You've got to protect us." In the play, he is the ordinary man, surprised that "every week a new look comes out", occasionally uncertain of his pronunciation, aggressively proud of his night-school education, yet moved to embarrassed facetiousness by his son's knowledge of France, perplexed by a world where "you stand on the street today and spit, you're gonna hit a college man."

The confident certainty of dramatic movement in this play seems deliberately and successfully counterpoised against the loss of certainty that is the play's main theme. The keynote of the play is its questioning. Dialogue in the theatre is regularly carried on in terms of questions and answers, but in *All My Sons* the questions are in effect dialogue-stoppers. The dramatic power resides in the sort of questions asked and in the invalidity of the characters to answer them. Particularly prominent in the last act and in the exchanges between Joe and his son, this is observable throughout, and it is responsible for the powerful climax to the second act in chris's agonized reiteration of such questions as "Where do you live, where have you come from ? ... What must I do Jesus God, What must I do ? "Nothing brings out Joe Keller's bewildered isolation better than this exchange with his wife:

Keller : May be I ought to talk to Ann?

Mother : Don't ask me, Joe.

Keller : (Almost an outburst) Then who, do I ask? But I don't think she'll do any thing about it.

Mother : You are asking me again.

Keller : I'm askin' you. What am I, a stranger? I thought I had a family here. What happened to my family?

Mother : You've got a family. I'm simply telling you that I have no strength to think any more....

Keller : Then what do I do? Tell me, talk to me, what do I do?[6]

A few minute later, among questions to his son, he interjects the same plea : "Talk to me", This is the bewilderment of a naturally garrulous man who has suddenly realized the impossibility of communication on the matters of deepest consequence and it is a dilemma which the often criticised banality of Miller's dramatic medium is particularly well suited to suggest. Against these baffled questions and the cliches of his grotidian conversation Joe's final statement the play stands out with an integrity and a force far in excess of its verbal content. His decision is made and his questions answered by the letter of his dead son. Looking at the letter in his hand, Keller says, "Then what is this if it isn't telling me? Sure he was my son. But I think to him they were all my sons. And I guess they were, I guess they were."[7]

This is almost the only statement in this play of questioning that should be taken at its face value and its quiet dignity makes Chris's summing up ("there's a universe of people outside and you're responsible to it") superfluous and gratuitously didactic. The other and more sensational statements must be seen in their immediate context. "This is the land of the great big dogs. You don't love a man here, you eat him : That's the principle" — it is not Miller who says this but Chris, and Chris, the baffled idealist in extremis. Its hysterical note distinguishes it from the more responsible tone of genuine recognition in Joe's speech, and the play is a social drama, not as an attack on the capitalist business ethic, but as a study of the bewildered common man groping in a world where moral values have become shifting quicksand, where you ask for guidance from others no surer than yourself and where the simplest lesson-moral responsibility to others—is the hardest to learn.

All My Sons is a realistic play illustrating the theme that a man must recognise his ethical responsibility to the world outside his home as well as in his own home."[8] A father's sin of producing shoddy war material for a profit results in the death of twenty one American pilots and in alienation of his family. Joe Keller, the protagonist, is faced with a choice between an aesthetic life in pursuit of heteronomous pleasure and an ethical life, which is attained by a self-determined acceptance of guilt and duty.

The economic upheaval of 1930's produced in Miller, the playwright, a strong social consciousness and drove him to examine the causes of society's evil and the individual's role in it. When Miller wrote *All My Sons* (1947), the economic depression has almost been forgotten and a world war had further jolted the foundations of a stable society based on family hierarchy. Throughout most of the Miller's work, the focus remains on the family, man, woman, two sons and their relation and responsibility to each one as well as society. Miller did share with Cliford odets a concern with socio-economic problems and he went ahead to examine them. This strain of social consciousness is American in original and can be traced back to the tales of Hawthorne as well.

In *All My Sons,* the hero Joe Keller represents this consciousness. His journey from self-to non-self makes the end of his quest. In *All My Sons,* the light is thrown simply on the social issues, in the tradition of the social problem plays of Ibsen, Shaw and Galsworthy. Miller regards the human situation as the product of forces outside the individual and the tragedies inherent in the situation as a consequence of the individual total onslaught against an order that degrades. He also believes that the function of tragedies is to reveal the truth concerning our society which frustrates and denies man his right to personal dignity; and the enlightenment of tragedy is the discovery of the moral law that supports this right.

In *All My Sons* the tragedy arises out of the character of his son, Chris Keller, out of an inner conflict between the affection of loyalty he had for his father and his concept of justice and universal brotherhood which the father offended. The persons in this play, however, exist mainly to illustrate the unhappy consequences of a disaster generated by a selfish materialistic society which respects economic success as it flaunts underlying moral law. At the climax of the play Joe Keller comes to realise that all the young pilots killed or endangered by his selfish action are his sons as much as are his own two boys for whom he was building up his business. In reply to mother's cry at the end of the play, "What more can we be" Chris, the surviving son, says "You can be better: nice and for all you can know there's is universe of people outside and you are responsible to it and unless you know that, you threw away your son because that's why he died" (p. 127). Really, Miller's concern with large social issues is the key of our understanding of the play.

Like most of Miller's dramatic figures, Joe Keller is a typical American. His suburban middle class background, his belief in the material success and in the family as the ultimate social and moral unit all make him a typical American. Like other tragic heroes of Miller, Keller is also committed to an ideal, however, narrow it may be, of family loyalty. He is a self-made man in business and has earned money for his family only. "What the hell did I work for ? that's only for you." (p.69) He assures Chris, who is thinking of driving away from house. He thinks in terms of the continuity of that materialistic success through his sons. "I want you to spread out, Chris, I want you to use what I made for you ... with joy. Chris, without shame .... with joy." His statement shows that he has committed the crime not knowingly, but vaguely in the nature of the risk taken by a man to whom nothing is bigger than a family and for this misconception he suffers and faces a tragic death in the end of the play. *All My Sons* is the author's contention that no individual's action can be self-contained, nor even within the campus of the family: Miller who wrote *All My Sons* with human understanding but moral sinew as well as taut dramaturgy summarized his theme as "the responsibility of man to society or the responsibility of man to his actions as a recognition of his ethical responsibility to the world and outside his home as well as in his own home."[9]

On the occasion of the premier of *All My Sons,* Miller declared in a press interview, "In all my plays and books, I try to take setting and dramatic situations from life which involves real questions of right and wrong. Then I set out, rather implacably and in the most realistic situations I can find the moral dilemma and try to point a real, though hard path out. I don't see how you can write anything decent without using the question of right and wrong as the basis." How well this statement applies to Miller's protagonist is clear when we read *All My Sons, Death of a Salesman, The Crucible, A View from The Bridge* and Miller's other plays. This also throws light on the range of his interest and the intensity with which he has pursued the twin concepts of truth and morality as highest priority in his work.

In *All My Sons* Miller points to our inseparable social responsibilities and makes it clear that any evasiveness or refusal is severely punished. Joe Keller's death is a parable of our times. Though Miller's works are appreciated by the critics for being free from any sort of preaching, he himself doubts and explains it rather in *An Introduction to the Collected Plays* by refuting that :

> "there will never be a satisfactory way of explaining that no playwright can be praised for his seriousness and at the same time he praised for not trying to teach the very conception of a dramatic theme inevitably means that certain aspects of life were selected and others left out, and to imagine that a play can be written disinterestedly is to believe that one can love disinterestedly"[10]

Miller was greatly influenced by Ibsen, he himself admit but he vigorously opposed the critics, comment that his plays have been influenced by Ibsen in their content and style. He says that Ibsen was important to him not so much for his master of the realistic form or for his ability to construct a dramatic fact from an idea and to make audiences listen to what he had to say. As a self-acknowledged playwright of social plays, one who defines social drama as "drama of the whole man", Miller also believes that society is inside man and man is inside society, and you cann't even create a truthfully drawn psychological entity on the stage until you understand social relation. In his more theoretical essays Miller again and again turns to the social relationship to stress that drama and the playwright, as exemplified primarily by Ibsen are reflections of the social barometer. Ibsen, Shaw, Chekhov, Brecht and Miller share in common the philosophy that the fate of man is social and that the stage should be considered as a medium more important for ideas than for mere entertainment, and should serve a serious purpose intellectually.

Miller appeared on the stage dressed in prophetic robes and clothed in a ponderousness. For Miller the true social drama, which he calls the "whole drama" must recognise that man has both a subjective and an objective existence, that he belongs not only to himself and his family but to the world beyond. This definition does not only fit *All My Sons* but also other famous plays : *Death of a Salesman, The Crucible* and *A View From the Bridge.* Miller, in one of his most important essays called "on social plays" has made his belief obviously clear that the serious playwright must write social drama. For him, however the genre is not simply "an arrangement of social evils". Gerald Weals accepts this belief that "the best of drama has always dealt with man in both personal and social contexts."[11] According to him a playwright should be concerned with both psychological man and social man. Miller's social dramas are inevitably forced with the problems of identity. This is what Miller has always written about and it is the subjects of *All My Sons, Death of a Salesman, A View From the Bridge* and *Incident at Vichy*. Each of Miller's heroes in these plays is involved in struggle which results from his acceptance or his rejection of an image of himself, an image that grows out of the values and the prejudices of his society. Although this preoccupation is found in Miller's other plays, it can be seen most clearly and effectively presented in *All My Sons*. The hero of that play, Joe Keller is a case in point. He is a good husband, a good father but fails to be the good man that his son Chris demands. His guilt in shipping out faulty airplane parts cannot be excused by his desire to save the family business, Joe does commit suicide. His death, however, is more than a single man's punishment for Joe Keller is a product of society. He not only accepts the American myth of the privacy of the family, but he has adopted as working instrument the familiar attitude that there is a difference between morality and business ethics. Joe Keller is a self-made man, an image of American success who is destroyed when he is forced to see that image in another context through the eyes of his idealist son. Joe Keller is a victim because he has attached himself to image his society has created and called good. The basic premise of *All My Sons* is that society is an image making machine, a purveyor of myths and prejudices which provide the false faces and false values which modern man wears. The implication is that the individual has little choice that he can conform and he destroyed as Joe Keller and Willy Loman are or that he can refuse to conform and be destroyed as John Proctor and Eddie Carbone are. These plays are not pessimistic because inherent in them is a kind of vague faith in man, a suspicion that the individual may finally be able to retain his integrity. This possibility appears most conventionally in the platitudes of Chris, the avening idealist of *All My Sons* and in the kind of death John Proctor dies in the Crucible. Joe Keller like Willy Loman has also wrong dreams that is to get a prosperous happy family by his own wrong attempts. And it is his own commitment to a pointless dream and his inability to simply walk away by throwing away all the family responsibility that have caused his disaster.

In *All My Sons,* Miller tries to create tragic drama of the Greek Genre in an age of the common man. His tragic characters are not at all exceptional, outstanding or bizarre. They are common decent men and the tragic flaw exists more strongly in the milieu than in them. They become, in a sense, the victims of external circumstances. But unlike, say, in Thomas Hardy, it is not "the cross casualty of fate" that plays the major role. Both the individual and the society are to blame. Miller presents man as the creature of society and at the same time as its creator. The individual and the society act and react on each other. Responsibility has to be jointly shared.

The elements of reversal and discovery have been skilfully handled by Arthur Miller. Till the announcement of George's coming, things are on the up and up. The sky has been cleared of all part clouds and the stage is set for a grand celebration in honour of Ann's return—suddenly the sky frowns and the situation grows more and more tense till Keller puts a bullet in his head. The anagnorisis, on the other hand, comes in stages. Even at the start, there is a strong suspicion about Keller's bonafides in the cylinder-heads affair. But plausible explanations are offered and we are lulled into serenity. Kate's warning to Joe at the end of the first Act that the boy is coming and he must be smart, puts us on the alert again. Even Ann is disturbed at the prospect of her brother's arrival. Keller insisting that a father is a father intrigues us further. George's revelation about the telephone conversation still more darken the pictures. And then Kate makes the slip and induces in us about the truth of Joe's Flu. Finally comes Kate's insistence that if Larry is dead, his father killed him. To us as to Chris, the enormity of the crime and the lie flashes suddenly. Larry's letter is the final nail on the coffin. The reason for his death opens everyone's eyes and we feel convinced with Keller that all of us are brothers, mutually responsible.

All My Sons therefore is a dexterously constructed Greek type tragedy in a modern setting. Theme of the individual's moral responsibility is timeless and timely. Joe's hamartia or lack of insight about what constitutes personal ethics triggers the tragedy. He is not a tragic hero in the classic, aristocratic sense but the magnitude of the tragedy is not to be defined in terms of rank and status. It is the spirit of the conflict that counts. The nearer the suffering man is to our station in life, the greater is his claim upon our sympathy. But for the grace of God, one of us might have been a Joe Keller. His tragedy therefore succeeds in effecting Catharsis in us.

It, must, therefore, be noted that Miller's strategy does not imply nihilism. Larry, the twenty-one pilots and Joe die. Steve goes to prison. But that is not the end. Life continues. The final curtain in *All My Sons* falls on Kate's exhortation to Chris "Forget now, Live". Individuals come and go, committing mistakes and paying for them. But life goes on. Nature works by trial and error.

All My Sons is the first essay in dramatisation of what may be a little man's tragedy. Miller in this play is not occupied with any of the three strains — the social, the Ibsenian and the tragic but in achieving the synthesis of the three, the diverse strains relating to the main American literary tradition of socio-moral concession. The European tradition of Greek tragedy are subtly blended in the play. In *All My Sons* the tragic balance is disturbed in favour of its social theme. It is significantly pointed out by Raymond Williams that *All My Sons* is a successful late example of the realistic drama and had its beginning in the domestic drama of the early 18th century and achieved its maturity in the plays of Ibsen by he rightly observed that in Miller's treatment of the experience of certain points its limits are reached.[12]

In *All My Sons*, the strain of social consciousness, the strain of Ibsenian realism and the strain of tragedy represent three distinctive traditions in dramatic literature. The way they have been fused into a meaningful unity is proof enough of Miller's originality and uniqueness as a dramatist. The coalescence, in fact, is so complete that no amount of discursive analysis can isolate the various constituents. In *All My Sons* Joe Keller represents social consciousness. His journey from self to non-self marks the end of his quest, "My only accomplishment is my sons" (p. 97), he says in the beginning. But before committing suicide, he says, "But I think to him, they were all my Sons. And I guess they were" (p. 126). The moral transformation of the hero is successfully dramatised in the play. Joe Keller is a prototype of the dishonest trader who worships success more than anything elso. He has been responsible for shipping defective cylinder-heads during the war, thus causing death of not only the twenty young persons but he also becomes the cause of misery of suffering of Deever, his neighbour and a business partner. Deever suffers physical torture in the prison house but more agonising is his mental torture which he has to undergo on account of his children turning away from him with anger and disgust. His children hate him and he is made in this way a scapegoat by the man on whom he bestowed his own faith. His partner Joe Keller turns his back on the days of his suffering and even does not bother to make any attempt on his own part. He realises his guilt only when his own son discloses the truth and abuses him in the presence of others. Being morally transformed by the anguish and suffering he faces, he is impelled to commit suicide. Miller here throws light on the life and attitude of the American people after war. Chris describes to Ann that life after the war is the same as it had been before — "that rat race again ... nobody was changed at all." It meant that those killed in the war had sacrificed themselves in vain. The value of cooperation and mutual responsibility which had been built by their actions had been lost and people behaved as if the war had been something like a "bus accident". Miller, the moralist performed his duty of a true artist, Chris, the dramatist's mouthpiece, seems to be exaggerating but the value of exaggeration lies in the idealism which is its positive side. It is related to the post- war disillusionment of both civilians and soldiers, those who survived after the horrors of war. They expected a better social order to emerge from humanity's experience in the war. Chris describes his feelings to Ann in Act I. After he hears his father defend his criminal action in the name of business and family. Chris says furiously; Is that as far as your mind can see, the business? .... Don't you have a country ? Don't you live in the world ?" Chris is here condemning not only his father but the short sightedness of the typical American businessman's creed. The play throws light on the humanist essence and the democratic nature of the playwright. Like Walt Whitman, he appears as an artist and intellectual who identifies himself with average life, understands it well and defends it with democratic fervour. He likes and appreciates manual work and neighbourliness and in the words of John Gassner, "he might be described as owning a kinship to Walt Whitman but maintaining a critical rather than rhapsodic attitude towards the life of our democracy."[13] Miller is certainly one among those writers who starting out as individualists, arrive at socialism and the preaching of social action .... Calling on man to merge into mankind. With a wide open heart he pleads through his writings for democracy and the common man. Miller's vision is existential, which takes note of the sense of anguish and alienation which common man is subject to. It probes still deeper into the mystery of life and ask questions about life, love, death and God. But even amidst despair and annihilation it perceives a moral order that exists in spite of all nullity and waste. This accounts for the existentialist's confirmation of sin and the Christian conception of piety and goodness in Miller's drama. Arthur Miller always takes full measure of the broken condition of modern man. Like Tennesses Williams, each one of his plays also embodies his particular individual inimitable vision of reality and his ultimate aim is to mirror the truth as far as he understands it. In this mode of approach, he is also quite close to Bernard Shaw. Miller believes that art is an imitation of the ultimate and external truth. Bernard Shaw has already declared his attitude towards life and art in the lines "My way of joking is to tell the truth. And this is the funniest joke in the world." Like Tennessee Williams, he communicates the essence of experience which is at once personal and universal, the growing complexity of the modern man, journeying through the dark and dismal phase of uncertainty through the outmoded technique of realism.

The central conflict of *All My Sons* like Miller's other earlier plays *Death of a Salesman, The Crucible, A Memory of Two Mondays* and *A View From the Bridge* grows out of a crisis of identity. The identity crisis is a crisis of consciousness. This is the heart of *All My Sons* and *Death of a Salesman* and Miller's other plays. The generativity crisis is one of conscience as well. In such a condition, as Dr. Erikson describes it, "the individual must face up to the fact that" I have done this or that ... my acts have affected others in this or that way. Have I done well or ill ? Can I justify the influence which intentionally or unintentionally I have had on others ?" This is the essential drama of all Miller's plays beginning with

After the Fall. It is the drama of some one who knows and accepts his identity and is conscious of his unique relationship to other people. The protagonists of Miller's earlier plays *All My Sons, Death of a Salesman.* struggled, for the most part unsuccessfully to discover who they were.[14]

Each of the protagonists in these plays is suddenly confronted with a situation which he is incapable of meeting and which eventually puts his 'name' in jeopardy. In the ensuing struggle it becomes clear that he does not know what his name really is: finally his inability to answer the question 'Who am I' produces calamity and his ultimate downfall. Strange, as it may sound, Joe Keller, Willy Loman, John Proctor and Eddie Carbone are alike, caught up in a problem of identity that is normally characteristic of youth and their deaths are caused by their lack of self-understanding. In every case this blindness is in large measure due to their failure to have resolved the question of identity as an earlier and more appropriate time in life. Miller presents this crisis as a conflict between the uncomprehending self and solid social and economic structure the family, the community, the system. The drama emerges either when the protagonist breaks his connection with the society. Miller sees the need for such a connection as absolute and the failure to achieve or maintain it is bound to result in catastrophe. He makes this very clear in his introduction to the collected plays where he writes:

> Joe Keller's trouble, in a word, is not that he cannot tell right from wrong, but that his cast of mind cannot admit that he personally has viable connection with his world, his universe or his society.[15]

All My Sons is a judgement of man's failure to maintain a viable connection with his surrounding world because he does not know himself. The verdict is always guilty and it is a verdict based upon Miller's belief that if each man faced upto the truth about himself, he could be fulfilled as an individual and still live within the restriction of society. But while Miller's judgements are absolute, they are also exceedingly complex. There is no doubt that he finally stands four-square on the side of the community but until the moment when justice must be served, his sympathies are for the most part directed towards those ordinary little man who never discovered who they really were on this point, a number of critics have made the point that Miller's Jewish heritage and the problems of life which he faced as a middle class man in a poverty-ridden family that depression brought to him, gave way to the subject matter of his plays and is one of the dominant motivating forces of his theatrical mode.

References

1. Dennis Welland, *Arthur Miller,* Oliver & Boyd, Edinburgh, 1961, p. 21.
2. Arthur Miller : Preface to an Adaptation of Ibsen's *An Enemy of the People,* New York, p. 17.
3. *Ibid.*
4. Robert Hogan : *Arthur Miller,* University of Minnesota Press, Minneapolis, 1964, p. 23.
5. "Preface", *Collected Plays of Arthur Miller,* Viking Press, New York, 1957, p. 306.
6. Arthur Miller : *Collected Plays,* Allied, New Delhi, 1973, p.119.
7. *Ibid.,* p. 125.
8. Garff B. Wilson : *Three Hundred Years of American Drama and Theatre,* Chap. 19, *Playwrights Between two world wars, University* of California, Berkley, 1959, p. 446.

9. John Gassner (ed): *From Henrik Ibsen to Eugene Ionesco,* Third College Edition, New York : The Dryden Press 1932, p. 1061.
10. Arthur Miller : *An Introduction to the Collected Plays,* Allied, New Delhi, 1973, p. 13.
11. Gerald Weals : *Arthur Miller, Man and His Image, American Drama Since World War II,* New York; Harcourt, 1962, p. 5.
12. Raymond Willams : "The Realism of Arthur Miller", *Critical*
Quarterly, (Summer, 1949), pp. 142-143.
13. John Gassner : *From Henrik Ibsen to Eugene Ionesco,* Third College Edition, Arthur Miller, New York, The Dryden Press, p. 1916.
14. Robert W. Corrigan (ed): Introduction : *The Achievement of Arthur Miller,* in A Collection of Critical Essays, Englewood Cliffs: Prentice Hall, 1958, p. 79.
15. Arthur Miller : *The Collected Plays,* Allied, New Delhi, p. 19.

3

The American Myth

(Death of a Salesman)

Willy : Do you know? When he died-and by the way he died the Death of a Salesman, in his green velvet slippers in the smoker of the New York, New Haven and Hartford, going into Boston— when he died, hundreds of salesmen and buyers were at his funeral...

Eugene o'Neill, the most dominant figure of the twenties, cast a long shadow on all the later dramatists. In the thirties Maxwell Anderson dominated the American theatre. In the forties and fifties, dramatists like Arthur Miller and Tennessee Williams took the American drama a step further. Miller and Williams were the most important playwrights of the post-war years in America. However, their plays reflect the milieu of the pre-war years. With Miller and Williams new horizons were opened.

> While William's imagination ran riot, Miller worked in a very austere framework. Miller was more after severe forms and serious themes than after

> the sensational. With almost ascetic restraint he esehewed whatever was out of his dramatic purview. Each character in his plays fights for self-respect and for the respect of his community, and for the public verdict of clean conduct.[1]

Arthur Miller explores the basic malaise of society, which is responsible for the nerve-racking tensions and worries of modern man. He views the individual not in isolation as Williams does but in relation to the environments. Though his moral earnestness sometimes sounds puritanical and old-fashioned the powerful dramatic elements in his plays make them interesting as plays.

In each of Miller's plays the individual has to confront society. Governmental authority, social authority and man- made laws are challenged and in their place individualism and natural law are glorified. Miller seems to suggest that the individual must protest against the injustice and the rigidity of society even at the cost of his life. By forfeiting one's right to protect, one will be committing a more heinous crime than suicide. Like Thoreau, he holds that one should not resign one's conscience to the legislator. Though Miller is constantly preoccupied with the individual and society, he betrays his metaphysical doubts. For, as Eric Mottram says, Miller finally has come to believe that "evil is really the natural cruelty of human nature, seen, not as a product of historical, social structures, but as inevitable data. The dilemma of his last two plays lies here in a nagging circularity which makes his work typical of frustrated American liberalism."[2] After Ibsen and Shaw, Miller is the only dramatist who has dwelt on the economic, social, political and psychological problems and still remained above them. In the words of Robert Brustein, Miller is a dramatist who "has the ambition to write a mature drama which transcends the family crisis, sexual conflict and the individual psychosis."[3]

When Arthur Miller began writing *Death of a Salesman* in 1948, he tentatively called the play 'The Inside of His Head'. The original title reveals much of what the play is about as well as about its structure. What Miller presents is a fusion of events in the present, in the past and in Willy Loman's mind. What Miller wanted to achieve was to make the structure reflect what was going on inside Willy's head. For this effect he used a blend of naturalism and expressionism which according to Benjamin Nelson, is successful because it "is mirroring the process of a disoriented mind."[4]

Death of a Salesman is concerned with the problems of the individual in fulfilling himself as a human being in modern society. The frequent references to the past illustrate the way of American society has changed during the course of the twentieth century. Three different parts of the century are contrasted. The earliest time is about the year 1910 when Willy embarked on his career as a salesman. Most of the play, however, is concerned with events in the present, that is, about 1945 and with these in 1928, the year most often recalled in Willy's dreams.

The references to the 1910 period and before relate to the American dream of creating a society in which each individual had the opportunity of living a rich and rewarding life. Willy's father had the satisfaction of making and playing the flutes which he sold as he travelled across the country. It hardly sounds a prosperous occupation but it suggests a freedom which is not possible in the city life of the present where one is at the mercy of one's employer.

The years following the First World War saw a rapid increase in industrial production. Products such as the refrigerator and chevrolet car mentioned in Willy's first dream conversation with Linda were made during this boom. Selling was still important but the salesman had no part in the making of the product now. The late twenties, however, brought the slump which caused high unemployment and shortage of money. It seems surprising that the Second World War is hardly mentioned in the play. There is only a brief comment by Stanley, the waiter. What is important is the ever-increasing mechanisation of society at this time. Machines have replaced men; craftsmen are disappearing : advertisements have become increasingly false : the population is growing to the extent of life being stiffled as suggested by the new apartment blocks preventing plants from flourishing in Willy's garden. The American dream of the U.S.A. being the land of opportunity for every individual is gone. That Biff feels this is suggested in his words, "Will you take the phoney dream and burn it before something happens?" Charley's example of the wealthy J.P. Morgan being liked only because he is rich also relates to the disappearance of personality as an essential ingredient of success.

In his 'Preface', Miller says, "I wished to create a form which...would literally be the process of Willy Loman's mind."[5] What we get then, is the contrast between 'I am Willy Loman' and 'He's just a guy', which is complicated by Willy trying to live by society's values. However, Willy confuses the new gods of money and power with the values of the past. His own values have, therefore, been corrupted, and we sense that his insistence on being well liked is not far from Happy's using his good looks to steal other men's women and this is also lined with Ben's advice. 'Never fight fair with a stranger' man as a victim in his society, as a man who can do nothing to change life significantly. In his Preface, Miller calls the play a contribution to the 'steady year-by- year documentation of the frustration of man'. That Willy feels this is apparent when he remarks to Linda. 'I'm not noticed, and Linda tells her sons when explaining Willy's breakdown, 'A small man can be just as exhausted as a great man.'

Escape from being just a little man seems to Willy to be through sporting prowess (in Biff's case), by leaving the country (as Ben did), or by accepting society's false values. Even the suicide act is seen by him in terms of money, the god of this society, but Willy's killing himself, mistaken as it is, does make him something more than the average American man. Miller writes in his preface.

> Had Willy been unaware of his separation from values that endure he would have died contentedly while polishing his car, probably on a Sunday afternoon with a ball game coming over the radlo.[6]

In response to Bernard's advice that it's sometimes better to walk away, willy asks, 'But if you cann't walk away?', to which Bernard says, 'I guess that's when it's tough'. And later as Willy makes up his mind to die, he tells Ben, 'A man cann't go out the way he came in.' Miller has written (in his Preface) that Willy has broken the unwritten 'law which says that a failure in society and business has no right to live'. This law he called the 'law of success'. Willy believes in this law and tries to live by it and this makes his tragedy the more intense, for as Miller goes on to say, 'to fail is no longer to belong to society in his estimate.' His position is made harder to bear because of his sense of responsibility to his family and the setting of the play in and around the house emphasises the importance of the family.

That Willy is normal rather than eccentric in wanting so much for his sons is supported by the interview with Howard wagner. Howard is equally obsessed with hopes and admiration for his children. Moreover, the fact that Howard himself seems insignificant and 'little' emphasizes the hold that modern society has over the individual even when he is rich. The wire-recorder has even been seen by some critics as symbolising the power of machines in our society, fascinating Howard to the extent of ignoring Willy while he excitedly talks of being able to record Jack Benny's comedy into radio show, and sending Willy into a panic as he turns the recorder on accidently.

The play indirectly makes a plea for a return to genuine friendship, to respect for the individual and to finding some way of satisfying man's needs in work that modern society with its synthetic, mass-produced, machine-made goods is ignoring. We may dislike Willy's ways of trying to succeed, but we should respond to his desire for respect for himself and his family.

> Miller's recurring themes are the relationship of the individual to society and the personal responsibility that the individual owes to society and the society failing the individual.[7]

'Evil', is the outcome of the conflict between the social pressure and the individual's will to succeed. ' The Man who had all the Luck' exposes a man's struggle in success. In *All My Sons* Keller says : "I am his father and he's my son, and if there's something bigger than that, "I'l put a bullet in my head." Miller tried to earn the sympathy of the audience for him and makes him a martyr to a false ethic of family and business sentimentality. His heroes are imperfect creatures, mean, boastful and selfish. By making them martyrs at the end Miller seems to have abused his artistic powers. But he says that he tries to "unveil a truth, already known but not recognised. The theatre can help to make man more human... that is, alone."[8]

In the *Crucible* Miller rejects the figure of the myth in economic and sexual reality. He tries to defend his heroes by saying that they refuse to 'settle for half" whereas in fact they do not deserve even that half.

Miller has consistently waged a war against sex even in spite of his marriage with the sexy screen heroine Monroe. Sex is a wicked influence for him. Willy's affair with women in Boston, Happy's seduction of the executives' fiances, John Proctor's adultery with Abigail in the *Crucible* all are made the basic evil of the characters.

> *Death of a Salesman* can be interpreted as an indictment of the modern civilization, to which millions of Lomans are becoming daily victims. The world presented here is full of aspirin, sacharin, chevrolets, studebakers, shaving lotions, refrigerators, stockings and washing machines and tape recorders of which none could cure Willy's troubles.[9]

They only added to his suffering. The more he had them, the more of them he wanted. Miller makes the meeting of Biff with his father in the presence of a tout the most crucial incident in the play. He traces the disorders of Biff's mind and the subsequent antagonism between the father and the son to this peculiar episode. Willy is subjected to perpetual torture and the son to this peculiar episode. Willy is subjected to perpetual torture by the appearance of the whore with whom he had an affair.

By stressing this incident, Miller is either betraying his puritanical traits or catering to the conventional taste. This is an age-old trick used by him to evoke tragic sympathy. "But sexual offence has, like the incest theme in 'Hamlet', lost much of its relevance to modern times."[10]

Miller may, perhaps, be showing that Willy is a double-faced role like the men of the sophisticated classes and this is what has disgusted his son. He may even be contrasting Willy with his son Happy who represents this class better. Willy is unable to forget the incident and his is plagued by a sense of guilt but Happy is blissfully free from this even though he has seduced the wives of a number of office executives. He would, without qualms, attend the wedding of the girls with whom he had slept. Here Miller seems to contrast those who take more animal pleasure in sex with those persons who suffer from feelings of sexual guilt. Willy is, however, able to live neither in his own world nor in the world of others which he envies. He is confused and he is not able to adjust himself to either.

Besides sex, Miller heaps up a number of disastrous elements to drive the hero to his doom. Willy is not able to provide for his son, he has lost his job, his wife has suffered too much, he is without a penny and he cann't grow a garden in the crumpted atmosphere.

His encounter with Howard shows another side of the problem in which willy is involved. Howard is a clever businessman and he seems to think that in business there is no feeling of gratitude or kindness. Howard is more interested in his children than in Willy who actually named him when he was born. He does not so much care for his father's memory as he cares for his children's recorded voices. But one cannot wholly blame Howard. he is disgusted with Willy's false pride. "Where are your sons?" he asks him, "why don't your sons give you a hand?" Willy boasts that they are working on a big deal. Howard who has understood Willy thoroughly by this time asks him to go and have a long rest. It is only Charley is his only friend, but still he feels jealous of him. When Charley offers a job, he refuses it. This disgusts Charley thoroughly. But in spite of this it is Charley who says the kindest word about Willy :

> Nobody dast blame this man. You don't understand; Willy was a Salesman. And for a Salesman there is no rock-bottom to the life. He don't put bolt to but, he don't tell you the law or give you the medicine. He's a man way out there in the blue, riding on a smile and shoe-shine. And when they start not sailing back... that is an earthquake. And then you get yourself a couple of spots on your hat and you're finished. Nobody dast blame this man. A Salesman is got to dream, boy, It comes with the territory."

Howard and Charley represent two different types of capitalism and Miller seems to be not so much concerned with ideology as with reality of character. In that the play is not so much a mouthpiece of either capitalism or communism. It only presents the way how the commercial society is making the individual more and more ambitious. This society has created only exhaustion, tiresomeness, nervous breakdown for the common man. His desires have become multiplied because there are more things in the shop to buy. Only a moneyed man can get anything he wants in this society. The fellow without money has only to gloat on them. Biff calls Willy 'a fake' but that is not exactly true. Had he been a fake, he would certainly have succeeded in the world. Everybody in this society worships fake values. "How to become rich by the shortest cut?" that is everybody's anxious question. Miller in bringing the downfall of Willy strikes at the very roots of modern society.

Willy is more interested in tending his kitchen garden than in farming. He is more after the garden in the enclosures of the posh houses than the countryside. He is oppressed by his surroundings and there is no place even for a kitchen garden. "There is not a breath of fresh air in the neighbourhood. The grass don't grow any more, you cann't raise a carrot in the backyard", he says. By this he doesn't mean 'going back to nature' or his love for rural life as some critics have interpreted it to be.

Death of a Salesman has a universal theme. It dramatized the tragedy of an obscure shoe salesman who makes false choices in life. and prepares his own destruction. "Attention, attention must be paid to such a person", says his wife to her boorish sons when she recognises the depth of his anguish. The power, the knowledge, and the sincerity of *Death of a Salesman* have persuaded millions of people to pay attention to the tragedy of this victim of the American social set-up.

The great success of this play in the United States is largely due to the self-identification of the Americans with Willy Loman and his problems. Though his set of values are ridiculous in the eyes of the Americans, they cann't deny, unwilling as they are, that these are the very values they live by and suffer from.

"The central theme of Miller", stated Dennis Welland, "has always been integrity... the integrity of the individual towards himself and towards his fellows... but the cost of that integrity for most of his characters has been life itself."[11] In the character of Willy, however, one does not find any integrity. Willy would have looked a lousy villain had he not been partially deranged. It is his schizophrenia that arouses our sympathy for him. It is also his schizophrenia that prevents him from becoming a successful man.

His schizophrenia is, in fact, related to his inability to practise the business ethics with all the burning and subtleties required. Temperamentally he is not fit for vile business though mentally he has dedicated himself to the ethics of the business world. He wants to do something which is not in his blood. He feels stifled in the midst of skyscrapers but still he wants one for himself. He is found of fresh air and gardens but business requires congested surroundings.

It is the conflict between Willy's temperament and the demands that the social honour makes upon it that brings about a tragic ending to his life. No physical or supernatural agency interferes with his life. The sense of disrupted privacy, the psychological neurosis, shatters him to pieces. Critics who think strictly in terms of Aristotle's obsolete poetics may not find Willy a tragic hero. To such critics Willy does not fall from great heights, he is a commoner and he lacks stature to be sufficiently tragic. To such critics Miller's answer is :

> "I would deny, on grounds of simple logic, that one of Aristotle's contentions if only because he lived in a slave society when a vast number of people are divested of alternatives, as slaves are, it is rather inevitable that one will not be able to imagine drama, let alone tragedy, as being possible, for any but the higher ranks of society."[12]

In the first instance we have to look on the phrase tragic hero with suspicion. In modern drama the hero has completely disappeared. What we find in modern drama is the common man or woman suffering as kings and queens used to suffer in the old drama. We have no tragic heroes or heroines but only tragic figures. Hence it is always safer to use the unambiguous phrase tragic figure in any discussion of modern drama. In *Death of a Salesman*, the protagonist is definitely a tragic figure if not a tragic hero.

To Miller the common man is apt a subject for tragedy in its highest sense as kings were. According to him, the tragic feeling is evoked in us when we are in the presence of a character who is ready to lay down his life, "if need be, to some one thing.. his sense of personal dignity. The passive who accepts his lot without realization is the person who is 'flawless'. Most man belong to that category."

The established view is that the fall of great man can excite pity and fear where as the fall of the common man... a man like ourselves... is not tragic but Pathetic. Great passions are only in great men. A king, for instance, can avenge his honour but a salesman has no honour to avenge, others argue that the impact of tragedy lies in our sympathetic identification with the hero and this is more likely to be achieved if the hero is like us. According to the democratic concept, all men are potentially great and therefore, their rank or stature is irrelevant to largeness of spirit.

"Tragedy", according to Miller, "is the consequence of a man's total compulsion to evaluate himself justly and his destruction in the attempt posits a wrong or an evil in his environment."[13] To him tragedy demonstrates the indestructible will of man to achieve his humanity. If a play can satisfy these demands, it is a tragedy irrespective of whether the hero is flawless or not, whether he comes from a high rank or a low rank in society.

The tragic state is the condition in which human personality is able to flower and realize itself. "The wrong, says Miller.

> "is the condition which suppresses man, prevents the flowing out of his love and creative instinct. Tragedy enlightens.. and it must, in that it points the heroic finger at the enemy of man's freedom. The thirst for freedom is the quality in tragedy which exalts."[14]

Has the playwright depicted any such exaltation in the case of Loman. Where? Miller says :

> It was not out of any deference to a tragic definition that Willy Loman is filled with a joy, however, broken-hearted, as he approached his end, but simply that my sense of his character dictated his joy, and even what I felt that his was an exaltation. In terms of his character, he has achieved a very powerful piece of knowledge, which is that he is loved by his son and has been embraced by him and forgiven. In this he is given existence, so to speak—his fatherhood, for which he has already striven and until now he could not achieve. That he is unable to take this victory thoroughly to his heart, that it

> closes the circle for him and propels him to death,. is the wage of his sin, which was to have committed him so completely to the counterfeits of dignity and the false coinage embodied in his idea of success that he can prove his existence only by bestowing power on his prosperity, a point deriving from the sale of his last asset, himself for the price of his insurance policy.[15]

Willy is the courageous soul "who cann't settle for half but must pursue his dream of himself to the end." Otherwise he would have died contentedly 'while polishing his car, probably on a Sunday afternoon with the ball game coming over the radio." Willy has broken an established law as Oedipus committed incest unknowingly. Even then he became remorseful and suffered from a terrible sense of guilt. Willy also has broken a law, and that is, he has failed in his business. Therefore, he has no right to live. This law has not been imposed on him by any outside power but it still is there in the society. He asks that unanswerable question. If Edision, Goodrich, Redgrange can make it, why not me?" Why not Willy Loman? This question is a general outcry and of fundamental importance and this is what keeps Willy's life on its heels. As this is not unique with only Willy and as it has become a general passion with every individual to succeed in life. Willy becomes the everyman. And that is what gets him the stature of a tragic figure. His weaknesses and his faults are the weaknesses and the faults of the modern civilisation.

Miller brings out the contradiction implicit in a democratic society most effectively in the life of Willy.

He is a man living in a society of confused values. Like every American, he, too, succumbs to the great American Dream in which the idea of personal success is of paramount importance. He is caught in the web of confused values... of opportunity, talent and fundamental right. Democracy which is sought after for the furthering of the well-being of the common man strangely confronts him and makes it less and less likely for him to succeed. Willy is a man trapped by his own culture.

Apart from such an economic and social statement implicit in the play, the play depicts a personal problem which Willy has to fight out for his existence. He is growing ineffectually old and his sons are not fixed up anywhere. They can neither live together nor apart from one another. Willy is a man of slipping powers locked up pathetically in the past and he has to seek fulfilment of an urgent personal need in the face of declining powers and approaching death.

In his review of the play's stage production in Feb. 1949, William Hawkins observed :

> *Death of a Salesman* is a play written along the lines of the finest classical tragedy. It is the revelation of a man's downfall, in destruction whose roots are entirely in his own soul. The play builds to an immutable conflict where there is no resolution for this man in this life.[16]

The play is a fervent query into the great American competitive dream of success, as it strips to the core a castaway from the race for recognition and money... The failure of a great potential could never be so moving or so universally understandable as is the fate of Willy Loman, because his complete happiness could have been so easy to attain. He is an artisan who glorifies in manual efforts and can be proud of the sturdy fine things he puts together out of wood and cement. At eighteen he is introduced to the attention he might receive and the financial vistas he might travel by selling on the road. This original deception dooms him to a life of towning and a habit of prideful rationalization, until at sixty he is far along his tangent that his efforts not to admit his resultant mediocrity are fatal. Through most of his career runs the insistent legacy of 'amounting to something' on his adopted terms, which he forces on his favourite son. With indulgent adoration, he unbalances the boy, demanding a mutual idolatry which he himself inevitably fails. If young Biff steals, it is courage. If he captains a football team, the world is watching. In the end, after repeated failure, Biff sees the truth, too late to really penetrate his father's mind. The boy's tortured efforts to explain his own little true destiny can only crack open the years—long rift and the salesman, with all his dreams' lost shadows, has no alternative to death for his peace.

> Unlike the dramas by Sophocles. Shakespeare and Lorca, Arthur Miller's *Death of a Salesman* is a tragedy set in our own times, played out on our own scene, by characters who, however we regard the quality of their thought, speak in our own language and with our own peculiar accents. In one sense, therefore, we cannot claim that the play is foreign to us. For what we lose

> of "Oedipus" because we are not Elizabethans and of Blood wedding by not being Spaniards, that much, at least, is ours because we are not Miller's American contemporaries...[17]

Centring on the quality of the protagonist, most of the comment about this play has argued the question of whether Willy Loman has sufficient stature to be a tragic hero. There is an irony in this debate over the admission of Willy to the company of Oedipus and Othello : few commentators have recognised the significance of the party's structure, of its use of scenes that embody and at the same time, illustrate the insubstantiality of the salesman's world of the smile and backslap : for the chosen structure indicates that Willy, though no less heroic—no less committed, that is, to his own dreams—is cast in different mould than that used for the traditional hero.

The Everyman element is, obvious enough in *Death of a Salesman.* According to A. Howard Fuller.

> If the salesman can properly be called the hero of American society, it would be difficult to discover a more fitting hero for a modern tragedy. For in a very real sense Willy, with his slogans and enthusiasms, is symbolic of the true spirit of a large, an important and one might say, a decisive segment of American life.[18]

Truly Willy Loman does represent any man whose illusions have made him incapable of dealing realistically with the problems of everybody life. He has sold himself by taking on an artificial personality that is wholly unrealistic. In pursuit of his delusions he ruins not only his private life but his career as well.

Mr. Miller's use of the expression Everyman would seem to offer a real due to the widespread popularity that this modern tragedy has enjoyed since its first presentation. Nearly everyone who sees it can discover some quality displayed by Willy and his sons that exists in himself and in his friends and relatives. It is this close identity between the audience and the characters that lends such poignancy to the tragedy. It cannot be duplicated by a modern audience when viewing the classical tragedies of the Greeks and Elizabethans.

According to Henry Popkin[19], Willy is much more emphatically a representative figure, an American Everyman, than any of Miller's other characters; accordingly, his problems are much less personal dilemmas than they are public issues. Willy is a useful instrument for Miller's social criticism. This quality of his is the first trait by which we identify this play as an example of Expressionism. Certainly this concern with large social issues is the key to Miller's definition of Expressionism in his Harvard Lecture ("The Family in Modern Drama", Atlantic Monthly, April, 1956) : "It is a form... which manifestly seeks to dramatize the conflict of either social, religious, or moral forces per se." In one of his articles, Miller finds that the Greeks and the Expressionists are alike in their efforts, "to present the hidden forces."

The hallmarks of Expressionism are its employment of symbolic characters. The man, the woman, the Nameless one (all three in Ernest

Toller's 'Man and the Masses'). Elmer Rice's Mr. Zero, Miller's Loman—and its presentation of dream states in which hidden forces of every variety become plainly visible. It was against the pioneer Expressionist, August Strindberg that Zola lodged the complaint that he did not know the last names of the characters in *The Father.* The characters of this play are Miller's Charley and Bernard in this respect, but no one complained about Miller's rootless figures. Perhaps the audience took it for granted that their name was Everyman. Certainly the acquired taste for Expressionism had made headway since the first American experiments in the 1920's. If Strindberg won the connoisseur's attention with *The Dream play.* O"Neill with *The Hairy Ape*' and Elmer Rice with *The Adding* Machine, what popular fame these writers earned rested on other plays. But with *Death of a Salesman.* Expressionism descended, in a slightly watered-down form, to the mass audience.

The Everyman theme is quite discernible. To locate the dream-elements of the play also requires no great effort. Willy Loman's dreams occupy half the play; they are the dreams of all the world, the dreams of a happy, hopeful past and the inescapable dream of past guilt. The recollections are not straight flashbacks in the manner of the films, but they are distorted, speeded up, heightened by repetition and selection. The accompanying music and the distinctive lighting of the original production compelled us to set these remembrances apart from objective reality. Further testimony of unreality is to be found in one figure who appears in them but seems to have no existence in the real world. Uncle Ben, the embodiment of the American will to suçceed. He is the fantastically rich relative who shuttles between the outposts of imperialism, Alaska and Africa. Long ago, he set out for Alaska to dig gold, he found himself on the way to Africa instead, and so he made his fortune in diamonds. When Willy last sees him, he is heading for Alaska. During the dream sequences, Willy seems unable to tell truth from fantasy, the present from the past. He loses himself in his recollections, interrupting a conversation with his neighbour Charley to address the absent Ben, losing all sense of the present in a men's room while he recalls his past exposure by his son. Willy is sick; his mental breakdown is certified by the hold his recollections have on him and by the great amount of obvious distortion in them. He has symptoms of Schizophrenia, but his sickness is not his alone. His identification with Everyman assures us that, as in other Expressionist plays, we are examining the malady not of an individual but of society.

Willy Loman's catastrophe is one of the poignant and inevitable misfortunes of our society and our time. The various formulations of the idea of success, whether created by Horatio Alger or Herbert Spencer or Dale Carnegie, have contributed to the state of mind that makes failure a crime. Success is a requirement that Americans makes of life. Because it seems magical and inexplicable, as it is to Willy, it can be considered the due of every free citizen, "even those with no notable or measurable talents. One citizen is as good as any other and he cannot be proved to be a natural-born failure any more than he can be stripped of his civil rights. The citizen may justly and perhaps even logically ask—if Edison, Goodrich and Red Grange can make it, why not me, why not Willy Loman? In effect, this is the question Willy asks his brother Ben. It is unanswerable ; the consequent disappointment that Willy feels is one of the great American exasperations. He postpones his anguish by transferring his ambitions to his sons and so the play's free use of time permits us to observe aspiration and failure in both generations. The problems, the exasperation, and the pathos of this family were sufficiently serious and important to make *Death of a Salesman* a moving play and a spectacular success. As a resourceful and understanding treatment of a critical human problem, this play makes an unmistakable claim upon us. But to examine it as closely as it deserves is to discover that Willy transfers his qualities and his characteristic confusions to the play itself. This is a very subjective play; it seldom takes us outside the ideas, the aspirations, even the vocabulary of the doomed salesman.

References

1. Dr. Murthy V. Rama : *American Expressionistic Drama.* Doaba House, Delhi, 1970, p. 73.
2. Eric Mottram : "The Development of a Political Dramatist", *American Theatre,* Stratford-upon-Avon Studies, 1967.
3. Robert Brustein : "Why American Plays are Not Literature", *American Drama and Its Critics.* Ed. Alan S. Downer. University of Chicago, 1963, p. 254.
4. Benjamin Nelson : *Arthur Miller : Pertrait of a Playwright,* Peter Owen, London, 1970, p. 108.
5. Miller, Arthur : *Introduction to Collected Plays,* Allied Publishers, New Delhi, p. 24.
6. *Ibid.*, p. 26.
7. Dr. Murthy V. Rama : *American Expressionistic Drama.* Doaba House, Delhi, p. 82.
8. Arthur, Miller : *Preface to Collected Plays.* New York,

Viking Press, 1957, p. 306.

9. Dr. Murthy V. Rama : *American Expressionistic Drama,* Doaba House, Delhi, p. 83.
10. *Ibid.*, pp. 83-84.
11. Dennis Welland : *Arthur Miller,* Oliver and Boyd, London, 1964, p. 26.
12. Arthur Miller : *Preface to Arthur Miller's Collected Plays.* p. 5.
13. *Ibid.*, p. 6.
14. *Ibid.*, p.7.
15. *Ibid.*, p. 7.
16. William Hawkins : "Death of a Salesman : Powerful tragedy: *The Critical Review.* No. 9, 1949, p. 202.
17. Judah Bierman, James Hart and Stanley Johnson : *The Dramatic Experience*, Englewood Cliffs, N. L., 1958, p.128.
18. A. Howard Fuller : "A Salesman is Everybody", *Fortune.* May, 1949.
19. Henry Popkin : "Arthur Miller : The strange Encounter". *American Drama and Its Critics—A Collection of Critical Essays*, ed. Alan S. Downer.

4

The Crisis of Conscience

(The Crucible)

Proctor : A fire, a fire is burning ! I hear the boot of Lucifer, I see his filthy face! And it is my face, and yours, Danforth ! For them that quail to bring men out of ignorance, as I have quailed and as you quail now when you know in all your black hearts that this be fraud—God damns our kind especially, and we will burn, we will burn together!

Arthur Miller's *The Crucible* makes use of history as allegory to depict a contemporary situation. The cold war between America and Russia following the Second World War, had created in America a widespread suspicion, and fear of communism. Senator McCarthy had set up a committee to investigate un-American activities and all over the country people began to suspect their neighbours, friends and colleagues. Miller himself was summoned under suspicion.

The story of *The Crucible* takes us back to the America of the seventeenth century when there was widespread fear of witchcraft. Under the dominance of the church several innocent persons were tortured and put to death. The hero of the play John Proctor is also falsely accused of witchcraft and there is a trial during which much of the evil and hypocrisy of the orthodox society are exposed. At the end when John Proctor is given a chance to save his life by signing a confession of his complicity, he chooses to be sentenced to death rather than implicate his name in a falsehood that will wipe out his identity. The play is thus more positive and heroic in tone than the previous plays. More clearly in *The Crucible* than in his earlier plays, Miller's aim is to depict man as the victim of a widespread evil in society over which man has no control.

At least three American dramatists in 1951 and 1953 wrote plays about the Salem witch trials, all of which were oblique comments on the mass hysteria that seemed again to be sweeping America. Of these *The Crucible* is the most celebrated; its first production ran for nearly two hundred performances and it has already achieved the status of a modern classic.

The Crucible might have been conceived as a tract for the times. But it is a play intrinsically valuable in its dramatic representation of a piece of life. And it is relevant to a recurrent situation in human affairs. As Benjamin Nelson points out :

> The crucible is topical. However, it is as pertinent to Inquisitorial Spain, the France of Robespierre and Danton, Nazi Germany and Stalinist Russia as it is to Mecarthyite America, not to mention Salem, Massachusetts of 1692.[1]

In *The Crucible* Miller dramatizes the principles of human behaviour inherent in a civilized society. John Proctor struggles to secure his personal dignity in the society and prefers to accept death rather than to live without a name. He is an ordinary farmer like an ordinary salesman in *The Death of a Salesman* who becomes the victim of existing social order. He is a true tragic hero. In his article, Arthur Miller argues that tragedies today may dramatize the predicament of a common man—" I believe that the common man is as apt a subject for tragedy in its highest sense as kings were."[2] Miller argues against the traditional association in the Western drama of tragic downfall with the figure of a king or a nobleman. In this regard, we find the influence of Ibsen on Miller's thinking and dramatic expression. The influence is certainly very profound and pervasive. In the 19th century the Norwagian dramatist Henrik Ibsen broke away from the traditional role by his writing like *An Enemy of the People* (1882), Rosmersholm (1886). All of them successfully proclaimed and proved that tragedy could be conceived around the lives of professional middle class men and women.

John Proctor is a modern tragic protagonist in Miller's view as Miller himself has stated his concept of the tragic hero in these terms :

> The tragic feeling is evoked in us when we are in the presence of a character who is ready to lay down his life, if need be, to secure one thing—his sense of personal dignity. From Orestes to Hamlet, Medea to Macbeth, the underlying struggle is that of the

> individual attempting to gain his 'rightful' position in society. Sometimes he is one who has been displaced from it, sometimes one who seeks to attain it for the first time, but the fateful wound from which the inevitable events spiral is the wound of indignity, and its dominant force is indignation. Tragedy, then, is the consequence of a man's total compulsion to evaluate himself justly.[3]

To be wounded by indignity, filled with growing imagination and to struggle in securing a personal dignity this is the essential core of John Proctor's experience. *The Crucible* however, achieves considerable complexity, as we have seen in view of the hero's efforts to gain his rightful position in a society where, because of fanatical devotion to orthodoxy, human values are perverted. *The Crucible* exposes a shameful period in American history when fanaticism destroyed reason and witch hunts reduced man to a fearful animal. Miller fights for the right to dissent.

The extent to which these definitions of tragic action characterize the play becomes clear to us when we go through the drama. We find that if the protagonist were willing to submit—that is, accept the indignity imposed upon him—he could survive as a man in the street without tragic significance. But, instead, he protests refusing conformity to the forces surrounding him and this makes him suffer. In other words, if he discovers—painfully, through experience —an individual course of action, he commits himself to this, and does so with such intensity that violence is unleashed against him.

This sequence of events, central to tragedies, may be expressed in Miller's own words :

> I see the process, essentially as this here is one, unlike most men; who quite unknowingly or with a certain degree of foreknowledge, acts at a moment when others would go silent or retire. In so acting he causes the scheme of things to react with retributive violence against him. It is a question of pressing the mechanism beyond its ability to exist in guilt. At bottom it is a questing after knowledge, a knowledge which is forbidden... His "fault' is that he lacks wisdom—he cannot let well enough alone, he cannot respect danger sufficiently.[4]

Proctor's intensity of commitment varies through the drama, as does the retributive violence inflicted on him. His questing after knowledge is a process of mind—a fluidity opposed to the rigidity of accusers and prosecutors—by which a degree of self-knowledge and integrity are ultimately found. Thus, the common farmer attains the tragic height by his questioning of values to secure the dignity of a private, innerly satisfying experience.

As is well known, tragedy portrays undeserved suffering without leaving us desperate or dejected or obsessed with a feeling of the worthlessness of life. The hero fails or dies, but in his failure or death there is a triumph. Pity and terror are evoked, but at the end there is calm of mind, all passion spent'. Tragedy shows us life in depth, provokes reactions about the significance and value of life and affects us to the roots of our being.

Judged by these criteria, *The Crucible* must be regarded as a fairly successful tragedy. Proctor's decision to die rather than buy life with a false confession is the catastrophe of the play. And the decision is preceded by agonizing soul searching. Till the very end, he has a chance to save himself. His choosing to die answers the question, "What shall it profit a man if he shall gain the world and lose his own soul?" His suffering and death are undeserved and he demonstrates the strength of a moral conviction that can defy death.

Proctor's minor lapse leads to developments which culminate in tragedy. A situation arises in which Proctor's passing infatuation for Abigail puts him in danger from which his virtues prevent him for escaping. Thus his weakness and his virtues function as parallel rails on which he is pushed to his doom. The essence of the tragedy lies in the fact that Proctor has to die because of his sense of responsibility to truth and to society at large.

The superstitious panic about witches in which Salem is plunged turns all values topsy-turvy. Normal standards of behaviours are overwhelmed in a mass hysteria which fancies seeing the hand of the Devil everywhere. When Proctor asks Hale how a charge of murdering children can be entertained against such a women as Rebecca Nurse, known for her piety and good works, he gives a reply which throws lurid light on the moral confusion in Salem. Hale says that even God had believed in the goodness of Satan till he started his revolt. In a similar vein, Parries points out to Proctor that the upright Cain became the murderer of Abel. Thus the people in Salem convinced themselves that anyone, whatever his previous record, may be a minion of Satan.

In this atmosphere, the only support for morality is one's own conscience, and when one's conscience is in conflict with public opinion, it must either be surrendered for winning safety or defied at whatever risk. The play shows Proctor wavering between these two courses. He cannot accept the assumptions behind the mass hysteria which affects Salem. Yet, he seeks to temporise with the law and the judges. He hesitates to reveal Abigail's admission to him in the early stages of the trials. When his own wife is arrested, he attempts to secure her release by submitting testimony in favour of her character and the evidence of Mary Warren disproving the allegations of Abigail. On seeing that the judges are sceptical about Mary's evidence. Proctor reveals Abigail to be an unchaste woman who had been his mistress. Even this confession fails in its objective with a view to saving his reputation, Mrs. Proctor declines to confirm it.

Proctor thus gets into prison charged as a sorcerer. For months he refuses to confess. At last, minutes before the time fixed for his execution, he offers a confession to the Deputy Governor. In making it, he is guilty of outright falsehoods. He saves his conscience by telling himself that he lacks the temperament of a martyr and that he has avoided confessing only out of pique and pride. But at the last moment, he realises that he cannot be true to himself by signing a false confession. If he does not feel like a martyr, he does not feel like a liar either. With a false confession nailed to the church, how can he ask his children to be upright and honourable? He is worried about his 'name'—that is, his integrity and his relations with God and the community. So he makes the choice to die and his death vindicates his name and censures the community.

Proctor's affair with Abigail is the remote cause of his death, while her malice and the superstitious panic which she can exploit are more immediate ones. His choice is necessitated by a past lapse and a painful dilemma involving it in part. He arrives at an understanding of himself through a bitter internal conflict. And that understanding makes it necessary for him to choose death rather than life. His spirit is strong enough to accept death deliberately and with open eyes. This acceptance implies neither despair nor any reflection on life as worthless. Proctor lives to affirm his faith in values—in truth to himself, to his community and to his God.

His death is undeserved : The mass hysteria which makes it necessary and which lets petty spite and private malice masquerade as pity and Christian zeal reveal the appalling depths to which human nature can sink. Still, the catastrophe is a triumph for Proctor and the values for which he stands. Even without learning from the post-script, "Echoes down the corridor", we feel sure that Proctor has won against his enemies who are also opposed to all that is good and noble. Rebecca Nurse, Giles Corey and his wife contribute to the same effect.

Thus in *The Crucible* we have all the elements of a tragedy-undeserved death and disaster brought about remotely by a minor lapse of the hero and immediately by an unusual situation which is exploited by his enemies, an internal struggle in which good qualities compel him to choose death and the affirmation for the values of truth and goodness by his choice. Pity and terror are evoked but the conclusion gives us an element of reconciliation by revealing the power of the human will to defy death.

The tragic effect is wrought by the struggle within Proctor and within the community. They are placed in a Crucible as it were and subjected terrific pressures. Thus the dross in them is burnt away and the gold is recovered shining and pure. The evil in human nature—its superstitions, malice and greed—is the fire that heats up *The Crucible* of the spirit : and the goodness is the gold that survives the fire. The name, *The Crucible* itself suggests that it deals with the purification and refinement of the human spirit which after all is the proper theme of tragedy.

Elder Olson regards *The Crucible* as one of closest modern approximation to tragedy[5], achieving its effect through the importance of the moral issues involved. This social tragedy creates a belief in the people that men, in spite of their error, are capable of enduring everything for their sense of decency. Miller has presented a number of heroes in his plays who suffer a tragic death. *The Crucible* has something of universal appeal in the exploration of complex relations between moral good and evil. The moral dilemma causes the immense suffering to Proctor who provides depth and intensity to this historical theme of Salem witchtrial, presented by Miller in modern context. Related to contemporary McCarthy hysteria, *The Crucible* reconstructs the Salem witchtrials of 1692 and therefore requires a lengthy exposition to establish the community's ethics, law and attitude. In the words of Miller himself, this play concerns true evil. The characters are like figures in a morality play, as is usual in Miller, but for the first time he shows the authority enacting its neurosis against the man who says, "No" to the law and "Yes" to his inner directing conscience. Proctor's final, "how can I live without my name" is the heartbreaking cry of man whose self-esteem had depended entirely on society. Moral climax reaches in Acts III and V. The action spreads from spring to Autumn and needs the sense of accumulating for its development. There are no flashbacks to dissipate suspense.

According to Valerie L. Barnish,[6] in considering the nature of tragedy and of a tragic hero, Miller takes issue with Aristotle's idea that a tragic hero should be of high rank, a dictum which he attributes to a slave society in which real freedom of choice is denied to all except the aristocrats. It should be noted that many Greek tragic heroes are more truly at the mercy of Fate than of wrong choices, and in such circumstances a fall from high rank may be advantageous in eliciting the tragic emotion. His hereos have pre-eminently a choice to make which will affect all their lives. The issues they face are of general importance and above all they face, as we all must, the fact of death, which Miller says, gives tragedy its lasting appeal.

In the Introduction to Collected Plays, Miller looks back at criticisms made of the play on its first appearance four years earlier. Some critics had complained that he had over-emphasized the malice and cruelty of the prosecutors, thus giving the impression that they were totally evil, monsters rather than human beings. Miller's reply is that the original records show them in exactly that light, that his presentation of Danforth, for example, makes him more human than the sources do, and that if he were to rewrite *The Crucible* he would intensify, rather than reduce, the evil nature of these men.

Miller's comments on how he might rewrite the play prompt one last question : what would be the difference between the play as we have it and the play as Miller suggests it might be? Miller argues that modern drama is weakend by what he calls "our inability to conceive of Iago.[7] He is referring to Shakespeare's *Othello*, where the villainous Iago, jealous of the noble and heroic Othello, wickedly and successfully schemes to destroy him by deliberately playing no the one weakness in Othello's character, his assumption that everyone else is as honest as he is himself. There is no doubt that Shakespearean tragedy affects us in a way that much modern drama does not. The ancient Greek philosopher Aristotle taught that tragedy performed the usual function of purging the audience's emotions of pity and fear. Othello certainly arouses pity for the hero and his wife and fear of the evil that Iago represents, but by the end of the play Iago is killed in punishment and our admiration for Othello's greatness counteracts our pity, so that tragedy has the paradoxical effect of restoring and perhaps strengthening our faith in man.

Now even if Miller were to rewrite *The Crucible* he could hardly achieve this kind of effect, however wicked he made the prosecutors because the historical facts of the story do not allow the prosecutors to be punished with the poetic justice that enables Shakespeare to kill Iago, and, admirable as John Proctor is in many respects, he cannot, as a simple Massachusette farmer, be given the heroic stature of a great leader and public figure like Othello. All this is relevant to *The Crucible* only because it shows us, by contrast, an essential aspect of the play that may indeed be one of its virtues. *The Crucible* does not end with the clearcut finality of Othello or the unmistakable restoration of order—the final stage directions have Elizabeth near collapse and Hale weeping openly; Danforth and Hathorne have not been defeated, although Proctor's courage is an important challenge to them; and the only ray of hope for the future is symbolized by the shaft of dawn sunlight that falls on Elizabeth. According to Dennis Welland,[8] the effect of this ending is not unlifting in the way that tragedy is, but neither is it totally depressing, and in one sense it may be more realistic. By not embodying evil in one Iago-like figure and suggesting its elimination by his death, *The Crucible* is a reminder of more insidious forms of evil that can be brought about by ordinary men. Such forms of evil are perhaps more obviously discernible in the modern world than is Iago's, and in that sense more frightening.

Several critics have made the point that *The Crucible* is not moving enough to stir us deeply. According to Walter Kerr, the play is only "a mechanical parable"[9] which prefers making points to creating characters. George Jean Nathan finds the tragedy " too remote from the heart."[10]

It will be unfair to these critics to take them at their word. Surely, they cannot mean that they are indifferent to the fate of John Proctor. Probably, they are merely informing us that the end of the play has not brought tears into their eyes, as some other plays have done.

In Shakespeare's tragedies, we can see that *Hamlet* and *Othello* are not of the same kind, that each moves us in a different way. The death of Desdemona seems to tear at our heart-strings more violently than the end of Hamlet. But the Prince of Denmark is no less a tragic hero than Desdemona a tragic heroine. If small things can be compared with great, we may say that Proctor resembles Hamlet more than Desdemona. He does not choose death in a rush of feeling. It is clear sighted reasoning that makes him understand that he cannot be loyal to truth, to himself and to his friends, if he makes a false confession in order to escape death. Such a decision cannot leave us unmoved.

As a political allegory *The Crucible* attracted a great deal of attention when it was first produced. Supposed to be an attack on senator McCarthy's campaign against communism, it was praised or condemned according to the political convictions of the critics. Howard Fast saw in the play an allegory of the trial, conviction and execution of the Rosenbergs who passed on some of the secrets of the atom bomb to Russia and praised it. Robert Warshaw denounced the play for misrepresenting the puritans in the dramatist's zeal for political criticism of contemporaries.

But it is oversimplification to say that play is a mere political tract. Miller's intention here is to write an ethical social play, that would be sharp, that would lift out of the morass of subjectivism, the squirming, single defined process which would show that the sin of public terror is that it divests man of conscience, of himself. The play undoubtedly has set for himself a high degree of ethical awareness and it is this what makes the play as excellent work.

The play is a parable only to the extent that it shows that the Salem trials throw light on persecutions and pogroms in totalitarian regimes and even in democratic societies when they are seized by panic. But surely, the characters in *The Crucible* are not mere mouthpieces of various points of view. Abigail, Parris, the Proctors and Hale are certainly lifelike characters. The dry bones of history get infused with life. The records of the trial contain statements and confessions, questions and answers. But in the play, the accusers, the accused, the judges and the community in which they lived become real.

While dealing with the nature of the drama, Miller himself admits his altered dramatic aim in *The Crucible* and says :

> *The Crucible* is internally Salesman's blood brother. It is examining the question I was observed with before the conflict between a man's raw deeds and his conception of himself; the question of whether conscience is, in fact, an organic part of the human being, and what happens when it is handed over not merely to the state or the mores of the time, but to one's friend or wife. The big difference I think is that *The Crucible* sought to include a higher degree of consciousness than the earlier plays.[11]

> In *The Crucible* the social and artistic approach of the writer is quite revealing. In the beginning, the primary aim of the play-wright is his consciousness of social and historical truths but as the play advances, by the choice of his moral design, Miller imparts a new meaning to it. Miller admits the form, the shape, the meaning of *The Crucible* were all compounded of the faith of those who were hanged.[12]

In *The Crucible*, thus, we find the three distinct strains, that is historical, social and tragic, merge together and by virtue of it he succeeds in creating a mounting tragic intensity.

The title of the play itself has allegorical significance. A crucible is a pot in which metals are melted down, usually in order to purify them by separating out baser elements that have become mixed with them. Using this as the title of his play, Miller implies a concern with a process of purging by fire. This is a familiar metaphor for man's spiritual improvement as a result of exposure to a period of great strain and temptation. Thus it identifies the spiritual development of John Proctor as the play's central theme.

An alternative explanation might be that Salem in 1692 was *The Crucible* from which there emerged a purified American democracy. Given Miller's interest in the historical and political aspects of the story, and his use of such phrases as 'the power of theocracy in Massachusetts was broken' this is by no means implausible, but the structure of the play would suggest that this association is only secondary.

There may, incidentally, be a slightly grim irony in this title. In popular belief, a normal place of a witch's equipment was a cauldron in which all kinds of unpleasant ingredients were brewed together for purposes of black magic. Shakespeare's witches in Macbeth use a cauldron and in Act One of *The Crucible* it is established that the girls had a kettle with them in the wards for a similar purpose. Miller's title may thus imply that a cauldron may become a crucible, that out of attempted evil good may come : this would be quite consistent with the themes of the play.

If we look at the different aspects of the work, *The Crucible* is found having all the qualities of naturalistic drama. When staged, the audiences found an appearance of real life in private homes, court house and prison cell. The heightened language of the dialogue, tending frequently to prose-poetry, may be declaimed to convey a sense of historical authenticity. Its relevance of moral crisis of New America and Salem society stands for all times and all places. *The Crucible* was not meant to be merely a mirror help up to the un-American Activities Committee but it is meant to explore pure evil in the words of T. C. Worsley.[13] Robert Hogan finds :

> The dialogue of the play, a considerable accomplishment. It suggests the flavour of 17th century speech without becoming distractingly archaic and without sacrificing simplicity, strength or suppleness.[14]

Robert Warshaw remarks "we must not be misled by its obvious contemporary relevance. It is a drama of universal significance." Further he adds, "It means, we should not be misled by play's historical theme into forgetting the main point, which is that witch trials that is always with us and specially today."[15]

Robert Warshaw logically proves the universal significance of the play, *The Crucible*. He says :

> What Mr. Miller is trying to say to us in this play ? It is hard to tell. In *The Crucible* innocent persons are accused and convicted of witchcraft on the most absurd testimony, in fact, the testimony, of those who themselves have meddled in witchcraft and are therefore doubly to be indicted. Decent citizens who sign petitions attending to the good character of their accused friends and neighbours are thrown into prison as suspects. Anyone who tries to introduce into the court the voice of reason is likely to be held in contempt. One of the accused refuses to plead and is pressed to death. No one is acquitted; the only way out for the accused is to make false confessions and join themselves the rank of accusers. Seeing all this on the stage, we are free to reflect that something very like these trials has been going on in recent years in the United States. How much like ? Mr. Miller does not say. But very like allowing of course

> for some superficial differences, no one has been pressed to death in recent years, for instance. Still, people have lost their jobs, for refusing to say under oath whether or not, they are communists. The essential pattern is the same, isn't it? And when we speak of universal significance, "We mean sticking to the essential pattern; Mr. Miller is under no obligation to tell us whether he thinks the trial of Alger Hiss or Rosenberg. Let us say, was a "witch trial" he is writing about the Salem trials.[16]

The play reaches its climax with John and Elizabeth Proctor facing the problems of whether John should save himself from execution by making a false confession, he elects finally to accept death, for his tormentor will not be satisfied with his mere admission of guilt; he would be required to implicate others, thus betraying his innocent friends and his confession would of course, be used to secure the hanging of the other witches. Now it is very hard to watch this scene without thinking of Julius and Ethal Rosenberg, who might also save their lives by confessions. Here the question arises, does Miller believe that the only confession possible for them would be a false one, implicating innocent people— Naturally there is no way for Miller to let us know. Perhaps he was not even thinking of Rosenberg at all. Then how can we blame him for what comes in our head when we watch the play? And if, we think of Rosenberg and Alger Hiss and others think of Prague trial, it proves the universal significance of *The Crucible.*

Miller wanted to write down what he apparently felt to be going on in American life today, so he took the help of an allegorical form and got success in his attempt.

All in all, Miller in *The Crucible* is not content with the writing of realistic social tract, he creates a universal work by fusing the realistic and the social with the poetic and the tragic. Miller's language in this play is more poetic than in *All My Sons* but is the quasi poetry of understatement, the poetry of inarticulateness. No one expects the use of uniformly poetic language even in a poetic play like *King Lear.* Miller's language becomes the language of heightened awareness, whenever the dramatic situation demands it.

Quite recently in an interview with Mark Lamos 'An Afternoon with Arthur Miller' when he was asked, "Is Shakespeare really the playwright of the possible ?" Miller answers, "I think that's true. But Shakespeare also had a mythology to draw on. I learnt how important that is in writing *The Crucible.* Where I had the history there, the myth to go back to."[17]

The Crucible derives its value also from the fact that its theme is not merely of historical or academic interest. It is of significance at all times and is of particular significance to us today. In the Preface to another play, Miller refers to the question whether one's vision of truth ought to be a source of guilt at a time when the mass of men condemn it as a dangerous and devilish lie. The courage to face persecution and to die for one's convictions is needed in every age. The play is not obtrusively didactic. But it portrays with dignity and reference the martyrdom of good men and women for freedom of conscience.

References

1. Nelson Benjamin : *Arthur Miller.* London, Peter Owen, 1970, p. 189.
2. Arthur Miller : "Tragedy and the Common Man". *New York Times*, 27 Feb., 1949, pp. 1-3.
3. *Ibid.*
4. Sheila Huftel : *Arthur Miller* : *The Burning Glass*, The Citadel Press, 1965, p. 113.
5. Elder Olson : *Tragedy and the Theory of Drama*, New York, 1961, p. 249.
6. Valerio L. Barnish : *The Crucible*, Methuen Paperbacks Ltd., London.
7. Arthur Miller : *Introduction to Colleted Plays.* Allied, 1973, p.7.
8. Dennis Welland : *Arthur Miller—The Crucible*, Longman, York Press, p. 42.
9. Walter F. Kerr : "*The Crucible*", From *The New York Harold Tribute*, Jan. 23, 1953, p. 12.
10. George Jean Nathan : *The World in Falseface.* New York, p. 119.
11. Arthur Miller : "Brewed in *The Crucible*", *The New York Times*, March 9, 1958, Sec. 2, p. 3.
12. *Ibid.*
13. T.C. Worsley : "American Tragedy", *The New Statesman and Nation*, August 23, 1958, p. 220.
14. Robert Hogan : "Arthur Miller", *University of Minnesota Pamphlets on American Writers.* p. 30.
15. Robert Warshaw : " The Liberal Conscience in *The Crucible*", from Robert Warshas : *The Immediate Experience.* New York, Doubleday, 1962, pp. 189-203.
16. *Ibid.*, pp. 139-203.
17. Mark Lamos : "An Afternoon with Arthur Miller", *The Sunday Statesman*, July 12, 1987.

5

Betrayal and Sacrifice

(Other Plays)

Quentin : God , why is betrayal the only truth that sticks !

Arthur Miller's *A Memory of Two Mondays* is a deeply felt piece of autobiographical nostalgia. "Nothing in this book was written with greater love", said Miller, "and for myself I love nothing printed here better than this play."[1] His satisfaction was understandable. He had found it possible, without resorting to turgid generalisations, farfetched 'myths' or abrupt changes in narrative direction, to define the predicament of characters who are unable to understand or combat oppressive influences in their society. By tracing its imprint in their lives, he had implicated an "industrial apparatus which feeds (men) in body and leaves them to find sustenance for their souls as they may."

In contrast to Miller's major figures in other works, the warehouse workers in *A Memory of Two Mondays* neither sustain with singleminded intensity their pursuit of personal goals nor despairingly seek release. For the grand outburst of a thwarted personality, the dramatist substituted unspectacular goings and comings of individuals divorced from all consuming commitment ; he "speaks not of obsession but of rent and hunger and the need for a little poetry in life." There is, therefore, no climax—a circumstance that may lead the reader to underestimate the emotional power of the play. Instead, there is a subdued movement from levity to sadness that recalls the alternation of moods practised in *All My Sons*, although in *A Memory of Two Mondays*, the humour has been exaggerated, the sorrow muted. Miller calls the play a "pathetic comedy."

The first Monday begins with the happy confusion of a farce. At one point, several employees try to revive sagging, stuporous Tom with face-washing and ear-blowing, with shouts, shakes and whiskey : at the same time they argue with one another, serve customers and placate the proprietor. "It's the same circus every Monday morning", the manager of the warehouse grumbles, giving the slapstick routine an apt. name. The characters are comic types appropriate to this burlesque beginning. Raymond, the ringmaster ; Tom, the perpetual alcoholic; Gus, a rowdy Falstaff; Jin, a truthful friend; Kenneth, poetic and aimless; Bert, innocent and wide-eyed Agnes, the nervous spinster; Patricia, the uncertain ingenue; and unhappy husband; a hedonistic bachelor; an insensitive employer; two young amartalecks; and a wonderfully ungrammatical mechanic.

The variety of accents emanating from this melange suits the humorous recreation of lower-class work-a-day life in a New York city automobile parts warehouse during the middle 1930's. As usual in Miller's writing, colloquial constructions make known a character's national origin, educational limitations and personal idiosyncrasies. On the second Monday six months later, the carnival hilarity gives ways to resigned sadness and cynical resentment. From force of habit, Gus incites the regular week-opening bedlam. "Look at them goddam mice I" he calls : "He starts rocking the scale... Patricia screams as mice come running out from under the scale. A melee of shouts begins everyone doging mice or swinging brooms and boxes at them." (Stage Directions).

But tired, good-natured old Gus, after his wife's death and twenty-two years at the warehouse, runs down at last; that night he ends his life "right". Larry, awakened from his dream of automotive glory, has sold his expensive car : "Funny how you get an idea, and suddenly you wake up and you look at it and it's like—dead or something. I cann't afford a car." Agnes has become more tearfully sentimental. Patricia's coarse : "Tom, sober, self-righteous and boring."

As the city's grim dims his perception of natural and human beauty, Kenneth testifies to the fading of hope. The sadly funny result of his crusade to wash the windows—he succeeds only in bringing into sight an adjoining brothel-underscores for him the futility of resisting mental stagnation ("Shouldn't have washed the windows, I guess", the boss observes). Deadened by monotony, Kenneth's mind lose its grasp upon his "chosen -image" of what he wants it to be. So he resigns himself to a dull future as a government clerk, concluding the play with his bittersweet song about a minstrel boy's romantic adventures. Only young Bert, more a spectator than a participant, escapes; the others attain at best a quiet maturity that enables them to endure.

The lack of a dramatic crisis is thus aesthetically just. "*A Memory of Two Mondays* has a story but not a plot." Miller comments, "because the life it reflects appears to me to strip people of alternatives and will." These characters do not suffer heroic disasters ; they are simply worn down by drudgery and grime. Their visions of fearer, happier life slowly fade rather than suddenly turn into nightmare. They become minor mechanisms in company and society : the warehouse symbolizes their corporate existence, the source of both despair and stability. The author notes in his stage directions that "it is a little world, a home to which, unbelievably perhaps, these people like to come every Monday morning despite what they say," To adapt a critic's remark in another context, Miller is concerned with two things : "the enmity of the machine age for the human spirit" and " the way humanity tries to persist through it."

If in most respects this is a minor play, it is clearly a minor play by a major playwrights who has learnt to coordinate all the constituent elements into a unified pattern. Thus the counterpoise of the two halves of the play, already suggested by the title is worked out simply but effectively by a see-saw relationship between two of the characters. Tomary, the drunken clerk of the first part, becomes, by a tremendous effort of will, the triumphant teetotaller of the second, while Kenny, at first a poetry- spouting, likably rough Irish idealist, has by the second part begun the process of regeneration into a drunken lout, though with flashes of the old decency still surviving. There is no direct causal connection between the changes that take place in the two men, they have no influence on each other, nor is there any significant interaction between them in the story. In the second part, however, we recognize a loss of vitality in both of them. The reformed Tommy has a priggish rectitude and hardness that are much less attractive than his earlier, if unregenerate, warmth : and the Kenneth who has turned to drink as an anodyne has lost the rugged spontaneity that he had at first. The passage of time is hinted at by these unobtrusive signs of ageing in all the characters in the second part. Realizing that Tommy and Kenneth have lost some of their earlier attractiveness, we realize that the other have also calcified a little. *The Two Mondays* earn separated by the time it takes a young man, Bert to earn enough money for his first year at college. It is through his memory that we see the warehouse, its occupants and the action of the play and thus there is no formal division into scenes. The continuity of flow suggests the unity of Bert's experience. And the time-gap is marked only by a short semi-lyrical exchange between Bert and Kenneth and a brief soliloquy, that is how Brett's memory sees it. With the exception of Tommy and Kenneth, it is not the characters who have changed so much as Bert, who has matured in his view of them. Moreover, Bert's exposure to experience is suggested adequately by the formal patterning of the play.

A Memory of Two Mondays is about many things. The play is a moral romance. It expresses a preoccupation with the facts that everything we do in this fragmented world is so quickly wiped away and the goals when achieved, are so disappointing. It is also the beginning of a further search and it lays the basis for a search. For it points the different roads, people do take who are caught in warehouses and in this play the warehouse is our world—a world in which things are endlessly sent and endlessly received, only time never comes back.

As Miller admits the play had been at the back of his head for many years. He had an ambition to write shorter and shorter plays as he believes, "it is harder to hit a target with one bullet."[2] For Miller, "There are perfectly wonderful things one can say in one sentence, in one letter, one look or one act."[3] His desperate attempt to do it is the result of the two plays *A View from the Bridge* and *A Memory of Two Mondays*.

A Memory of Two Mondays is a pathetic comedy, a boy who works among the people for a couple of years, shares their troubles, their victories, their hopes and when it is the time for him to depart, he expects some memorable moment, some sign from them that he has been among them, that he has touched them and been touched by them. In the sea of routine that swells around them they barely notice his departure. Miller here describes that subculture where the sinews of the economy are rooted, the darkest Africa of our society from whose interior only the sketchiest messages ever reach our literature or our stage.

Obviously the author's preference for the play has its basis in certain reminiscences, while others plays of Miller are indirectly related to themes that have haunted the memory. This one-act play expresses directly the experience of an intelligent youngman doing manual work among a group of people.

> The play has been shaped out of autobiographical material and it explains the writer's fondness for the play which, in fact, touches the very core of the problem of modern tragedy. Miller believes that decline of the individual and its interest in the modern industrial society which is due to its fragmentary nature has compelled him to centre more and more on his private life.[4]

The relationship between a man's identity and the image that society demands of him is a rearing theme of Miller's plays. In *A Memory of Two Mondays*, we come across the crisis of an individual acceptance and rejection of an image that is the product of his society's values and prejudices. It is obviously the effect of depression that Kenneth one of the characters of the play expresses himself:

> Kenneth : Why, it's the poetry how, Gus, don't you know that? This is the hour all men rise to thank God for the blue of the sky, the roundness of the everlasting globe, and the cheerful cleanliness of the subway system. And here we have some axles.

In this world of dreariness, nothing is new and exciting for these groups of people. Even their jokes confirm their inner frustration and suffering. There is, of course, more than pathos in the statement. The old hardy ribald Gus, impelled to carouse all weakend because of twenty-two years of accumulated monotony from the warehouse, yet obsessed with the guilt by having been carousing when his wife was dying, awakens our emotion stronger than pity. He draws all his money from the bank and goes on a last great spree, buys a suit of clothes rents three taxis simultaneously, drinks, makes long distance calls to all his friends and finally dies in one of his taxis. Automobiles were the cross of Gus's life, but he did die with some heroic bravado. Gus's life just as fully squashes him as Willy Loman's did to him. He has also his burden of guilt, but he has a vigour about him, an indomitability.

A Memory of Two Mondays has a universal appeal. Miller remarks, "it was meant to be a leaf of bread for people when I thought they were getting sick with cake."[5] John Gassner rightly finds *A Memory of Two Mondays*, "a sensitive and admirably uncontrived genre piece."[6] Robert Hogan also finds Miller "able to pack so much in so effectively." For Hogan "in a way it is like trying to pack the 'Plough and the Stare' into one act and succeeding. This is a moving, technically adroit and beautiful job, one of the rare, instances of a one-act tragi-comedy."[7]

The protagonist of *A View From The Bridge* acts in a specific, social milieu that conditions his sense of guilt and his sense of dignity. Yet for Eddie Carbone guilt and dignity derive from an intimate attachment. His fatherly concern for his niece is as obsessive as that shown by Joe Keller and Willy Loman for their sons, his dramatic existence as dependent as theirs upon filial allegiance, his grief after being deserted as sharp. His reactions answer the question, to what lengths might a man go to protiect his prerogatives as a father? "I want my respect !" Eddie shouts, repeating the demand made-often with the same words — by Miller's chief characters.

As in earlier plays, too, the 'subjective reality' of the protagonists trial assumes central artistic importance. For the first time, however, in *A View From the Bridge* sexual desire and jealousy become the dominant components of that reality. Eddie's fervant insistence on his niece's loyalty carries with it an implication of physical attraction. Eddie refuses to accept such an application; but, like Willy Loman and Joe Keller, he involuntarily bores his emotional secret with his words and actions. From the beginning of the play his extreme possessiveness suggests the strength of a passion he will not acknowledge. The thought that Catherine could be contaminated by the world's wickedness or subjected to another man's authority is intolerable to him. Morbidly sensitive about her claim to adulthood he dislikes her short shirts and clacking high heels, her 'wavy' walk, her chats with Louis and her plan to get a job. "You're a baby", he insists, though she is almost eighteen: "I guess I just never figured on one thing.... That you would ever grow up."

But Catherine has grown up, and her feminine maturity represents a potential threat to the innocent, affectionate rapport between uncle and niece. Beatrice, Eddie's wife, detects this threat. She feels obliged to warn the naive girl not to throw "yourself at him like when you were twelve years old", not to appear "in front of him in your slip", not to sit "on the edges of the bath tub talkin" to him when he's shavin' in his underwear." "It's wonderful for a whole family to love each other", she argues, "but you're a grown woman and you're in the same house with a grown man". Alfieri, a lawyer, refers more directly to a sexual motive : "Sometimes", he tells Eddie, "there is too much love for the daughter, there is too much love for the niece." Eddie's agitated responses to such statements attest to his unwillingness to admit the presence of this motive. "What're you talkin' about, marry me! I don't know what the hell you're talkin about! 'furiously' retorts, after Alfieri states, "She cann't marry you, can she?" And Eddie is "shocked" and "horrified" when Beatrice puts the problem quite bluntly : "You want something' else, Eddie and you can never have her." Eventually, in drunken jealous rage, he expresses in gesture the secret he had denied in speech : "he reaches out suddenly, draws (Catherine) to him and as she strives to free herself he kisses her on the mouth."

Miller was particularly interested in the decisiveness of this inadmissible but irresistible passion — "a passion which, despite its contradicting the self-interest of the individual it inhabits, despite every kind of warning, despite even its destruction of the moral beliefs of the individual, proceeds to magnify its power over him until it destroys him. "The principal narrative convention" Miller uses to "manify its power" is a love triangle. The rivalry rises immediately upon the entrance of Rodolpho and Marco, brothers who have just illegally entered the United States from Sicily, in a scene that splendidly illustrates Miller's ability to encompass strong anxiety in common-place place talk. After the introductions, Rodolpho gradually dominates the conversation, impressing Catherine with his exuberant charm Eddie had addressed his first remarks mainly to Marco, the elder brother then, eclipsed by the younger, he speaks progressively fewer lines. This reticence, together with the defensive nature of his occasional comments, subtly indicates his grown uneasiness and resentment. Finally, as Rodolpho crowns his dazzling self-exhibition by signing a popular lyric, Eddie abruptly terminates the song and the scene by reminding his guest of his uncertain legal status as an immigrant. "Now" Alfieri declares, making the point explicit, there was a trouble that would not go away." Except for this declaration, the inception of the sex-rivalry is conveyed entirely through Eddie's ominous silences and through the connotations of his sullen dialogue.

Eddie's subsequent responses reveal the depth of his turmoil. He insists that Rodolpho is an irresponsible "hit-and-run guy" who wants to marry Catherine only to obtain American citizenship — he is an 'enemy' and a 'thief' who breaks into a home, "makes a stranger" of its head and tries to carry off its treasure ("he's stealing from me !"). This accusation, however, inaccurate is not nearly so far-fetched as the next, that the blond Rodolpho must be a homosexual as well as a thief. After all, he cooks, sews and sings "in a high tenor voice." "I mean he looked so sweet there, like an angel you could kiss him he was so sweet." Eddie enmeshes himself so completely in his delusion that he impulsively tries to prove it to his niece by kissing Rodolpho before her. The grossness of this act and the irrationality of his accusations, which could have no effect other than to further alienate Catherine, indicate the intensity of the longshireman's desperation.

Shame and hopelessness drive Eddie to a still more irrational dead: seeking to protect his family's integrity, he destroys it. He violates the Sicilian code of honour operative in his social world by betraying the brothers—and, unintentionally, the relatives of a friend to the immigration authorities. Disgraced now both in his neighbourhood and in his home, he hazards a last defence of his 'name', in the manhood ritual of the duel with Marco, then is delivered from humiliation by death.

A View From the Bridge may thus be seen as an intriguing psychological study that shows the self-destructiveness of an inflexible, passionate individual. As such, the play resembles *All My Sons, Death of a Salesman* and *The Crucible.* Again, however, Miller hoped to enlarge his scope beyond that of psychological analysis. He worked toward this end with Alfieri's commentary and with the vendetta between Eddie and Marco. As narrator, Alfieri, a contemporary substitute for the Greek chorus, establishes a rhetorical contrast with Eddie much greater than that Chris and Joe Keller.

Death of a Salesman was written "in a mood of friendly partnership with the audience", *A Memory of Two Mondays* with personal love. "Miller creates in *A View from the Bridge* a modern tragic drama out of a story heard years before, with an attitude "of passionate detachment."[8] In *A View from the Bridge* Arthur Miller deals directly and heroically with the problem of betrayal. This is a play about an informer and all else is secondary to that fact and just as in *The Crucible,* Miller sought for and found a classic American setting, so here does he take out an ancient Italian and human condition. The play is family representative.

Eddie Carbone's incestuous desire for his niece Catherine, places the play in the company of Greek Tragedy. In-capable of either rationalization or evasion, the hero finds himself caught between an ancestral code and a sexual passion whose remotest implications he fails to know. Blindly he is driven to break with the primitive code and suffers bloody revenge at the hands of his fellows. Since his passion involves the rejection of his wife for his niece, a kind of incest and a shocking scene in which his niece's lover is accused of homosexuality. There is a danger that the audience might find more titillation than tragedy in the play.

In the words of Robert Hogan, "the play seems an attempt to utilize the austere technique of Sophocles in a modern setting, just as Maxwell Anderson's *Winter-set* was an attempt to do the same thing with the manner of Shakespeare."[9] *A View From the Bridge* echoes both Sophocles and Shakespeare, when we go into the depth of the play. Eddie Carbone's blindness for his own incestuous desire for Catherine is Hamartia, or the fatal flaw that brings the hero to his death."[10] The tragic integration of his personality is like Shakespeare's Lear. These literary echoes from the Greek and the Elizabethan classics indicate a powerful trend in modern drama. Like Eugene O' Neill and T. S. Eliot, Miller also, by echoing the theme and the structure of the Greek dramatists, imparts a more lasting universal touch to the ephemeral nature of his realistic theme. Eddie's dramatic personality gives tragic intensity through the process of disintegration. But the question arises "disintegration of what?" In order that a dramatic figure attains tragic richness by fall, he should first attains 'height'. Does his suffering strike a responsive chord in the heart of modern audience? How far is the sordid behaviour consistent with the sublime nature of tragedy? There are a lot of questions regarding Eddie Carbone's being a tragedy. In such attitude to the question raised is that of Arthur Gunj who assessed the personality of Eddie in terms of 'Stature', a 'remorseless fate' and 'shoddy crime'. His statement that Miller has not tried to make Eddie significant by making him a man of heroic stature or by setting him against a remorseless fate, but by giving him especially in his revised version of the play, a kind of innate self-admiration ("underserved since Eddie has, in fact, been guilty of a very shoddy crime)"[11], betrays his admiration for the traditional tragic hero conceived in Aristotelian terms and his condemnation of the modern naturalistic theme as a fit subject for tragedy. Such attitude as this, is also that of Richard Findlater, who considers Eddie Carbone unfit or as the hero of the tragedy, no matter how modern the dress or how democratic the century."[12]

Miller retains the terminology of Aristotle's *Poetics* but invests it with new meanings. In modern society where the individual has to struggle against the evil that resides in society (environment), there is little relevance of tragedy emanating from a Aristotelian "tragic flaw". Miller thus reverses the meaning of the "tragic flaw". Rather than be a flaw, it becomes a virtue in so far as the common man as a tragic hero is concerned. "Tragedy, then, is the consequence of a man's total compulsion to evaluate himself justly."[13] Rightly, in his plays, the social evil has replaced the Greek force of distiny that descended heavily on a protagonist every time he made the slightest departure from the moral law.

Bamber Gascoigne rightly affirms that "The power of the play is in the Wild power of Eddie himself. He is a man possessed, as a man who refuses to settle for half and he reveals yet another recurrent theme of Miller's that of the tragic obsession."[14] However, he regards the play as only nearly tragic.

Miller in this play is confronted with the problem of bringing about a fusion of the classical and the naturalistic. He largely succeeds in the double tasks by the fusion of the two versions of realistic techniques - the American realistic technique of O' Neill and the German epic realism of Brecht.

> The creation of Alfierie in the play is a novelty for Miller which consists in his resemblances with Tennessee Williams Tom in The Glass Menagerie, the narrator of the play and also a character in it.[15]

Alfierie combines in himself the double orientations. As a narrator in the likeness of a Brechtian figure, he introduces the major persons in his immediate American setting as well as universal antecedents, appears at crucial and decisive moments in the life of the protagonist and plays a vital role in the development of dramatic crisis. Secondly, he acts as 'chorus' and by offering his comments on the role of the hero, becomes an authentic mediator between the author and the audience. By his help Miller saves the play from the danger of opportunistic sensationalism and lack of the appreciation of audience.

After the Fall is the most introspective play that Miller has written. It has assumed the form of an interior dialogue, a progress in self-discovery accomplished without a psychiatrist. "This play", Miller wrote in the Foreward, "is a trial; the trial of a man by his own conscience, his own values, his own deeds. The Listener (an unseen character addressed by Quentin, the protagonist) who to some will be psychoanalyst, to others God, is Quentin himself turned at the edge of the abyss to look at his experience, his nature and his time."

The chief symptom of Quentin's malaise is loss of faith in self and in others. Having held the naive belief that "underneath we're all profoundly friends." Quentin was severely shaken by disloyalty among husbands and wives, acquaintances and business associates. His own affairs proved exceptionally disappointing. He was "admired", honoured "blessed", "loved" and "adored"; yet he found these good-damned women have injured me. And he inflicted injury as well as received it; indeed, he wonders if he has "lived in good faith." The evidence of "good faith" that he reviews is not encouraging. He felt neither indignation nor compassion during a visit to the site of a Nazi extermination compound. His coldness rebuffed Holga, Louise and Maggie. It drove his present fiancee to fears, his first wife to psychotherapy and his second wife to suicide. Even his attitude towards his mother was ambiguous. He honestly loved her — so much in fact that he was criticised for it. Still, after he died he said, "I can't even mourn my own mother. It's monstrous ... I don't seem to know how to grieve." The only woman he remembers without unpleasant associations to Felice, whose enthusiasm he did not reciprocate... I have lived through all the promises, you see ? He concludes: "I am bewildered by the death of love. And my responsibility for it."

This bewilderment concerning sincerity was complicated by the contradictory titles others gave him. On the positive side, his mother saw him "a light, a light in the world", and later admirers compared him to a "pasha", "grand duke", "king" and "God". Negatively, he was called a merciles 'judge', a 'little boy', an 'idiot', a 'fraud, a 'stranger' and 'a son of a bitch'. "But where is Quentin?" he asks, "do you know who I am ? .... I cannot find myself." He ponders over the angry remark his father had directed to him as a youth: "Chrissake, what are you?" His goal now is to "stop impersonating" to go "disguised no more" and to "show what Quentin, Quentin ... is!"

The self-analysis follows a traditional pattern of psycho-analytic treatment. Dispirited by maladjustment in his personal relations, the subject seeks to understand the nature and origin of that maladjustment. He reviews significant events in his childhood and in his adult history for clues. Finally, he perceives the cause of - and hopefully, the cure for - his inadequacies. Quentin's disorientation had its roots in his youth; two memories, both of which show his mother to be "treacherous"; indicate he was impressed early with the instability of family relations.

Quentin's mistrust of intimacy led him to a predicament in which the desire for independence ("be a man") militated against the need for solace ("like a boy !"). Despite his pessimism, Quentin requires love: gestures and words of affection occupy a commanding place in his recollections.

Quentin recalls facts about his two marriages that illustrate this predicament. While he urged his first wife to express herself freely, he remained guardedly "distant" (Louise protested, "the moment I begin to assert myself it seems to threaten you."). He agreed that he had not been "very demonstrative" that "in seven years we had never had a meeting". Still, he could not keep from 'resenting' her rigid self-righteousness. Because of his resentment, Quentin ironically brought about the outcome he had feared. Instead of comforting him, Louise ended by blaming him — as his mother had blamed his father — and dismissed him with the same contemptuous exclamation spoken by both Mother and Folsie, "what an idiot" ! By the time his marriage foundered, family life had come to mean for Quentin the inevitable "death of love", for estrangement always seemed to follow intimacy.

At this juncture he encountered Maggie-again. A beautiful creature unencumbered by moral and intellectual preconceptions, she seemed to offer the perfect cure for his condition—simple, unselfish, inexhaustible idolatry. "You're all love , aren't you?" he inquired, "that's all I am !" She responded. Unhappily she was extremely neurotic about love, partly the result (as with Quentin) of childhood traumas. Maggie never know her father; after a pathetic attempt to locate him, she adopted Quentin as a father-surrogate of infinite wisdom and honesty (You're like a god !").

But the wedding ceremony was hardly over before she exhibited her 'forbidden side', and insatiable appetite for total devotion—just what Quentin could not give. Soon her 'timid idolatry' changed to wrath, exposing Quentin once again to a woman's scorn. Gradually in his wife's eyes he metamorphosed from a father-figure into an 'idiot', or an 'ogre' symbolizing "all the evil in the world". Maggie's "flash of contemptuous anger" iterated Louise's earlier repudiation, Mother's growing contempt for father and Eleio's sudden flash of contempt for Lou. The hostility between Maggie and Quentin marked another completion of the recurring cycle in which love, at first freely proposed was then selfishly withdrawn; a cycle in which fidelity, hopefully sought, was soon bitterly lost.

During most of his odyssey Quentin thought himself more sinned against than sinning. He considered both wives guilty of "pride"—one vain about her virtue, the other vain about her sexual attractiveness. He did glimpse his unconscious "hypocrisy" and "fraud" in "playing God". Not until his self-analysis, however, does he fully comprehend the extent to which ego, the power of self-assertion and of self-preservation, has directed his motives even when they were ostensibly altruistic. "I loved them all!" he realizes, "and gave them willingly to failure and to death that I might live". He then understands the truth in Louise's notion that "we are all separate people". This understanding serves as his guide to sanity. He will "dare to love this world again", but now love must be tempered by the humbling knowledge that any individual would "kill" those he holds dear to ensure his own survival. Quentin's quest for his real identity turns up a killer as well as a lover.

In *After the Fall*, Miller dealt with his local themes of faith and meaning within the confused national and personal life of America and dealt with them without obstructions which might call for a rethinking of the great society. It is the first of Miller's plays where the main emphasis is almost personal. It is also the first of Miller's plays where the largest part of the action concerns itself with martial relationships.

Here Miller is attempting at a synthesis between "sufficient real psychology and a full feel of the real world"[16] and is trying, as he himself states, "to relate the subjective to the objective truth."[17] For the dramatic projection of this complex theme, he resorts to the use of Strindbergian technique of dream like seemingly at random progression and association. This dream technique is adequate for upholding the psychological progression in Quentin in relation to his home, his friends, the women he loved and the mass destruction of war. But alongwith this adoption of the Strindbergian dream technique, there is also in this play "Ibren's feel for structure and for point."[18] The technical brilliance of the play consists in its attempt at fusing the two divergent technique of Kaleidoscopic vision, dream progression and association and the Ibsenite technique of retrospection leading inevitably to a moral point.

After the Fall is Miller's self-revolution and a trenchant comment on the nature of profit, necessity and American moral behaviour in mid-century—a re-working of *The Crucible* in contemporary terms into which he worked his own American confusions of public and private life. The play is also a comment on how sexuality had become a convention in the theatre, 'a kind of shorthand through which we can appear into lives of people, we're seeing." He also intended to teach Americans, traditionally fancying themselves 'open handed, on the side of justice, a little bit careless about what they buy, wasteful but essentially good guys, optimistic, about their under-level, the level which confronts our bewilderment, our lonely naivete, our hunger for purpose.'[19] The play also concerns itself with the difficulty for locating 'the forces of disintegration' in the personality striving for integrity.

In this autobiographical play the characters are recognizable, for Miller life has long been public property-Miller, the writer is Quentin, the lawyer; Marilyn Monre is Maggie, a cabaret singer and even Elia Kazan who directed the play for the Lincoln centre, is the friend who names his comrades before the un-American Committee is his friend Nicky. Miller has unveiled each and every personal detail and submits his innermost self to the world.

Harold Clurman finds *After the Fall*, "signal stop in the evolution of Arthur Miller as man and artist."[20] Morris Freedom says, we may read *After the Fall* alongwith *Death of a Salesman, All My Sons* and *The Price* as a kind of Galsworthian tetralogy, an integrated saga in which there is a thematic progression. The play may be read, indeed as a work about the same family considered under changing circumstances and from different perspectives. The development from the first play to the fourth play provides a record of some of the changing values of American middle class family life during the period in which they are written."[21]

In an essay entitled "Our Guilt for the World's Evil" Miller attributes the factual basis of *Incident at Vichy* to a story he heard from a friend. In 1942, a certain Jew (Leduc in the play) was arrested in Vichy, France, which though still unoccupied was subject to Nazi racial policies. As he waited to be interrogated, together with others suspected of being Jewish, he realized that a death sentence was inevitable. Before his turn arrived to enter the police office, however, a Gentle suspect (Prince Von Berg in the play) who had just been freed enabled the Jewish prisoner to escape at the cost of his own life. The story came to signify to Miller nor the heroism of the Gentle nor the suffering of the Jew but the inhumanity and 'common want of solidarity' of both: "what is dark if not unknown in the relationship between those who side with justice and their implication in the evils they oppose". Von Berg, 'the hero of the play' sides with justice. He 'comes into the detention room with his pride of being on the human side, the right side.' Yet he (like Leduc) shortly discovers "his own complicity with the force he despises." Miller's lesson is that "it is immensely difficult to be human precisely because we cannot detect our own hostility in our own actions. It is tragic, fatal blindness ...."

In this play Miller's analysis of the human hatemechanism proceeds almost entirely along discursive lines. Leduc, a psychiatrist explains, "Jew is only the name we give to that stranger" within everyone. Recognition of this "stranger" would threaten one's sense of purity and power, so each individual finds it necessary to blame someone else for his own inadequacies : "each man has his Jew, it is the other". The 'other' — a visible embodiment of death and degradation — can be purged from the social body. Indeed, it is a positive if not holy deed to do so. Lebeau, a Jewish artist shows the effect of this attitude upon the scapegoat : "they keep saying such terrible things about us and you cannot answer. And after years and years of it, you .... I wouldn't say you believe it, but you do, a little .... You get tired of believing in the truth." (Leduc adds, more pointedly. "We have been trained to die"). As long as man chooses not to tolerate his fallibility, sacrificial murder "will be repeated again and again forever." But murder is negation, "and that is why there is nothing and will be nothing." Leduc states, to quote words spoken by a German major, "There will never be persons again. What do I care if you love me ?" By refusing to countenance his destructiveness, man becomes infinitely destructive. "I am only angry", Leduc Laments sounding the key idea postulated also by Quentin in *After the Fall* "that I should have been born before the day when man has accepted his own nature: that he is not reasonable, that he is full of murder, that his ideals are only the little tax he pays for the right to hate and kill with a clear conscience."

"What can ever save us?" Von Berg despairs, as the discussion moves from diagnosis to prognosis. Leduc tells the nobleman that there "will be nothing - until you face your own complicity." To affirm their 'humanity', men must charitably accept their common failing and selfishness. The humiliation resulting from this acceptance can be meliorated by exchanging 'guilt' for 'responsibility'. Salvation for Miller's characters lies in self-knowledge.

Leonard Moss says that "Miller's characters in this play whether blind or visionary; are merely vehicles for theoretical assertion."[22] The blind, frozen in their respective postures, refuse to admit their 'implication in the evils they oppose'. Each jealousy defends his accustomed identity, denies the worth of his brother and proves that "the Jews have their Jews". Leduc cannot find 'meaning' in the attitudes of friend or enemy.

Before their epiphanies, the prince and the psychiatrist take leading roles in the futile debate. Von Berg, an aesthete, interprets Nazi terror not as a meaningless accident, a capitalist conspiracy or a personality test, but as an "outburst of vulgarity". Leduc sees his position delimited in argument with the Austrian aristocrat, the Jewish actor and the German officer. Then Leduc and Von Berg attain insight —as in all Miller's plays, moral growth offsets moral rigidity and Von Berg carries out the play's only significant action in giving up his life for his friend. Yet the process by which the two attain insight receives little attention. Leduc suddenly perceives his own enmity after a momentary urge to take 'vengeance' on his wife ("what scum we are !"), the Prince understands his 'complicity' as abruptly when his tolerance for a Nazi cousin is pointed out to him. At last we can say that Miller has certainly verified his ability to portray mental complexities attendant upon "the fear of being torn away from our chosen image."

In *Incident at Vichy* Miller closes in on the crucial question of guilt and responsibility in a dialogue between a Jewish doctor and an Austrian Prince, detained by mistake, who believes himself to be a moral man. The doctor wrings from the prince an admission that he has "somewhere hidden in his mind, a hatred for the Jews" and that each man has his Jews — "including the Jews."[23]

Incident at Vichy repeats Miller's usual theme of self-knowledge under the pressure of forces both temperamental and environmental. In *All My Sons,* the awareness of evil is blinded by Joe Keller's passionate attachment to his loyalty to the family. The narrow walls of loyalty to the family suddenly collapse under the weight of his direct responsibility for the death of all the victims of the air-crash. The self-awareness of evil impels Joe Keller to commit suicide. The suicide of Willy Loman is the expression of tragic helplessness in Willy which transcends the limitation of material success. John Proctor's heroic resistance to the social evil becomes convincing only in the historical context of the play. The agonizing awareness of evil in Quentin in *After the Fall,* in spite of his depth in probing is too passive to save Maggie. The freshness of *Incident at Vichy* consists in the play's capacity to transform the sense of guilt into responsibility.

Eric Mottram believes that "the climax of *Incident at Vichy* is an act of courage and love within the context of nihilism."[24] He further finds that this nihilistic despair controls the belief and emotion of the play. Robert W. Corrigan assesses that:

> "the ending of Incident at Vichy reveals that otherness is an ambiguous reality. Without it there can be no promises and hence no love: but, at the same time, its very existence calls forth the murder which each of us carries within himself."[25]

Incident at Vichy like *The Crucible* is a kind of play that is bound to receive its dispassionate treatment with the distancing of time. It is a triumph for Miller in a fresh direction and is likely to be acclaimed a minor classic. It breaths an air of freshness and austere simplicity. The play has an overwhelming impact as an exciting drama of ideas. The historical background of Nazi occupation of France is largely responsible for the divergent assessment of the play by contemporary critics, writers and press reviewers. Douglas Watt of the Daily News attacks the play on the ground of its contrived theatricality and claptrap philosophy." But at the same time critics life Howard Taubman of the *New York Times* shower praises on this play. According to Howard Taubman, "Miller has written a moving play, one of the most important plays of our time ...." *Incident at Vichy* is a drama of towering moral passion ... it is a thundering cry of anguish that might issue from the heart of a prophet."

It is Miller's concern with life's balance of payments that he explores in his play, *The Price.* At the end of *After the Fall,* as Quentin goes to join Holger, he asks himself, "Is the knowing all?" Is the ha nd-won awareness enough? *Incident at Vichy* answers these questions, and the answer is "No! it is not enough". We must also, as Leduc puts it "make part of myself what I know", and we must make others come to see this truth. The great insight of *Incident at Vichy* is that we fall in this because of our inability to accept the otherness of people and, more important, because our guilt ridden nature will not permit anyone to acknowledge our own otherness. Locked in the prison of self, our guilt demands that there be a price — no free giving like Von Berg's — because then solipsism (egotism or extreme subjective idealism) becomes intolerable. It is this solipsism which makes us incapable of love, which makes us treat other and our relationships with them as commodities, as objects which, to use Merton's words again "can be used, exploited, enjoyed and then cast off." This guilt is first revealed in our insistence that "vengeance be mine", Leduc sees this attitude in his relationship with his wife and can acknowledge it to Von Berg because he still believes in his moral superiority over the Prince. But when Von Verg freely offers his own life to save the Jewish doctor, Leduc's essential guilt of which his vengeance is symptomatic — is fully expressed.

In *The Price,* Miller develops these themes further. This play, while longer than *Incident at Vichy,* is written with the same tight simple form and in it he returns to the family as the locus of the action. The play consists essentially of the confrontation of two brothers who have been estranged for sixteen years. Each of them has reacted in different ways to the terror provoked by their father's failure in the depression and has now returned to the old family brownstone to sell the parents' possessions before the building is demolished, Victor, a policeman with twenty-eight years on the force, has chosen the security of a humdrum but safe existence, justifying his and his wife's sense of failure on the grounds that he has sacrificed his own ambitions to take care of his broken father, Walter, on the other hand, while less talented than his brother, has became a famous and wealthy Surgeon. He is a selfish and egocentric man who sacrificed everything and everyone to his drive for success. At the same time, he is also an extension of Quentin and Leduc. A few years earlier he suffered a mental breakdown and has come to realize that because of his terror or failure he has, in effect, murdered life. He returns now, having seemingly and at long last conquered his guilt, to reestablish a relationship with his brother, who he believes has found a more meaningful existence through a life of self-sacrifice.

As the two men confront each other and their past, which is presented in all of its accumulation through the furniture of the set—each of them comes to discover that he represents a different aspect of the same dilemma. Miller puts this very clearly in his production note to the play, where he writes:

> As the world now operates, the qualities of both brothers are necessary to it; surely their respective psychologies and moral values conflict at the heart of the social dilemma. The production must therefore withhold judgement in favour of presenting both men in all their humanity and from their own viewpoints. Actually each has merely proved to the other what the other has known but dated not face. At the end demanding of one another what was forfeited to time; each is left touching the structure of his life.

The structure of life which both men are forced to accept as their own is a structure in which all of the positive aspects of otherness have been excluded. They have touched neither each other nor the world because they were not brought up to believe in one another but to succeed. In developing this idea, Miller is doing much more than challenging the whole American money ethos as he had in *Death of a Salesman.* This is a play about absence and the absence, at the core of the play is the absence of love. There is nothing at the centre of these man's lives and there never has been; there is nothing at the centre of Victor and Esther's relationship; there was nothing at the centre of Walter's broken marriage; there was nothing at the centre of their parents' relationship or in the sons' relationship to their parents. The great revelation of the play is spoken by Walter, when he says to Victor :

> It's that there was no love in this house. There was no loyalty. There was nothing here but a straight financial arrangement. That's what was unbearable.

The whole agony between the brothers hinges on the assumption that "There is such a thing as a moral debt." Both men have justified everything that they have or have not done, as well as everything that has or has not happened to them in terms of this imperative. This is particularly true of Victor. His wasted twenty-eight years are his moral capital, and, until Walter finally forces him to acknowledge that in his heart he knows he has been living a lie, he has managed to believe that this capital was backed by the hard currency of self-sacrifice. This feeling explains both his insistent need to demand 'a price' and also his need for vengeance even if it costs his (symbolically) his life. Certainly Esther has supported him in this belief, for their empty life together would have had absolutely no meaning or justification if there were no valid moral indebtedness. Walter, on the other hand, realized during his illness that he had paid the price and why he had done so. Now struggling with his guilt, he comes—again with a reasoning similar to Leduc's —to act : "I have learned some painful things, but it isn't enough to know: I wanted to act on what I know." What Miller is challenging, however, is the whole idea of moral debt based on 'Price'. For whenever people try to relate to each other in terms of the price to be paid, they will always get less than they bargained for, the price is never enough. Both Walter and Victor have been wrong; in life there can be no question of success or failure or "I gave more than you." This is the significance of Gregory Solomon, the used furniture dealer who has come to purchase the junk heap of their past.

Solomon, wisely enough thinks that it is silly for the brothers to worry about the price because it will always be fair. Whether the final price offered for the furniture is $ 2.50 or $ 25,000 really doesn't matter since as he says, the price of the used furniture of our lives is only a viewpoint and we can never deal with life's real issues in terms of quid pro quo. In addition to pointing up the fact that paying the price, but so what ? — Solomon's presence serves two other important functions. One of these is especially clear in the second half of the play. After dominating a good share of the first act, the old man is shunted to the bedroom shortly after Walter arrives on the scene and the second act is primarily devoted to the conflict of the brothers. But Solomon does not disappear altogether, and each of his entrances is significant. In effect, he serves to keep the brothers honest; his interruptions deter them from arriving at false or illusory solutions.

Solomon's other major function may be discerned in the numerous references to his daughter's suicide which are woven throughout the play. The first time his daughter is mentioned her suicide is not brought up, but simply the fact that she had nothing significant to believe in ("You're worse than my daughter! Nothing in the world you believe, nothing you respect—how can you believe?) In equating Victor with his daughter, he is prefiguring the emptiness of the policeman's life. And when Solomon continues, pointing out that if you cannot believe in the life you are living, then — "my friend you're a dead man!" the parallel to Victor is even more apparent. Finally he says about his daughter : "I had a daughter, should rest in peace, she took her own life. That's nearly fifty years. And every night I lay down to sleep, she's sitting there. I see her clear like I see you. But if it was miracle and she came to life, what would I say to her?" Then he " turns back to Victor, paying out."

Solomon has lived life fully and he is also a wise man. The essential lesson he has learned is that the murder or suicide in each of us can never adequately explain or justify what we have done or have not done to others. We must accept our guilt moving that it is just, but also with the full awareness that any attempt to seek revenge on others for the guilt for which we are responsible is to choose the road of nothingness.

The Creation of the World and Other Business is meant to be a comedy but with a serious message. It depicts the story of Adam and Eve's expulsion from the Garden of Eden for disobeying God. Their children Abel and Cain also live in mortal fear of God because of the wrong committed by their parents. Finally Cain kills Abel in an act of madness.

Miller ridicules the traditional belief rooted in the myth of the Garden of Eden that man is fallen by nature and that he has to atone for the 'sins' committed by his forefathers. Miller's point of view is that the 'fall' was a trick played on Adam and Eve which they could not understand. Similarly, Cain does not act out of evil, as is commonly believed, but out of fear of God. This play shows that Miller is trying to break fresh ground in experimenting with new forms and themes.

The Creation of the World and Other Business provides evidence of the American playwrights' continuing interest in the material of the Genesis. Miller himself tells us that he has been slowly awakening to the importance of representing the dramatic action through a myth :

> I think my plays are getting more and more mythological : the people (characters) are becoming less and less psychological. And perhaps it isn't as obvious to others as it is to me that characters in all my other plays are also mythological.

However, the use of the actual myth merely helps Miller to further clarify and crystallize his understanding of the human life as variously depicted in the earlier plays. The myth of Eden embodies life's meaning and complexities in an abstract and pure form, and Miller, like the other playwrights finds it easier to project his view of human condition through a re-adjustment and reinterpretation of the original situation of the myth.

Specifically, Miller is concerned in this play with two or three basic aspects of human life. First is the issue of man—God relationship which is essentially spiritual and includes the role of evil (represented by Lucifer) within that relationship. In this context, the focus is on God's personality and mind, and His motivation in enacting the drama of the 'fall'. Secondly, and this must be Miller's main concern, is the issue of man's relationship with other men, especially in view of the fact that all of them are 'fallen'. In this regard the factor that human beings, because they fail to be embodiments of intended perfection, should feel guilty, becomes important. Perhaps even God is not perfect because something went wrong in the act of His creation. And as a result of these considerations, man must learn to live in understanding and forgiveness. Discarded and disowned by God, man must depend on himself and other human beings to make life tolerable.

As the play begins, Adam and Eve are shown as living animals. They can hear the cry of the injured branch of a tree, hear the sound of the sunset and the cracking of a shadow as it moves on dry leaves. In their superficial contentment with the so-called perfection of their lives, they declare their appreciation of the greatness of God and of the perfection of His creation. More than anything else, the so-called perfection of the creation is embodied in the innocence of the Adam and Eve. That's why they won't eat the forbidden fruit. God, however, is worried because He has seen a flaw in His creation. It is that Adam and Eve are supposed to multiply but because of their innocence, they don't. Thus, ironically, the chief manifestation of God's perfection (innocence) turns out to be the main flaw in His creation.

Lucifer, appearing as the consciousness of Gods imperfection, remarks: "You've got to thin out the innocence down there" and "the problem down there is that you've made it all so perfect." But God is adamant because He has a strong reason against giving knowledge to the humans. "The more they know, the less they need Me." Thus motivated by self-interest, God refuses to let knowledge come to Adam and Eve. Lucifer's decision to tempt Eve is far from being an act of evil; it is intended to carry out God's purpose and make man complete.

With this muddle as background in the creation, Adam and Eve finally taste the apple. It makes them feel ashamed, ask questions about their existence and to some extent feel guilty of their disobedience. Thus the original sin becomes the primary cause of man's guilt.

The play which starts as a comedy with Adam and Eve's innocent quarries and Lucifer's tongue-in-cheek remarks on God's folly, remains quite entertaining up to this point. Thereafter, it develops into a serious situation in which Adam and Eve and Cain and Abel struggle to acquire a sense of direction and identity but without much help from the creator. In this part, an argument also emerges questioning God's motives in finalizing man's personality as based on fear of death and guilt of his own evil.

In fact, it is God's character on whom rests the outcome of the dilemma which has two levels. One is God's own level at which His problem is how to choose corrective measure so that His creation doesn't prove absolutely worthless and that Adam and Eve and the subsequent race of humans remain inalienable. The second dilemma is of the family of Adam in which they have to seek reconciliation with their own evil (dramatized by Lucifer) but also with the presence of calculating and manipulating and later, indifferent God. In this context, therefore, the personality of God that emerges is somewhat like this : He is mostly an angry God who threatens to wipe out the world — "burn it, flood it or leave it as dead rock spinning in silence" — if His authority is repudiated by the humans. Lucifer has a clear grasp of God's intention when he says that it is "to make them guilty and to put the fear of God back into them." Towards this purpose, God would first deny them the fruit of knowledge and after their expulsion, endeavour to put the fear of death in their hearts. The third act is therefore, a long exposition of God's scheme to bring about a 'death' so that mankind in future turns to God through their guilt. The Angel of Death Azarel is asked to blow visions of death when Adam's family are asleep. Cain, the most devout God-loving of Adam's family is spurned by God so that in his anger and jealousy he may kill Abel, his brother. Abel's death thus appears to be engineered and prearranged by God's manipulation of their minds and actions. The purpose of God's intentions seems to have penetrated into Cain's mind when he tells his parents that instead of living (after expulsion) as though they were blessed, they should be living in shame and guilt, begging for His forgiveness.

It is in the last three or four pages that the message of the play comes through. Eve's vehement protest that she doesn't understand what has happened Cain has killed Abel as if to prove God's superiority over Lucifer and God has walked away leaving Adam's family to its own fate-verges on an existential dilemma. The irrationality of the whole situation sharpens her anguish. It is at this point that Adam concludes the action by uttering the words which seem to represent Miller's ideas: "Cain, we are surrounded by the beasts! And God's not coming anymore. Boy, we are all that's left responsible— ask her pardon." And then turning to his wife — "Call to him, Pardon him. In God's name cry mercy. Eve, there is no other." The ringing cry for mercy and forgiveness and tolerance is the universal cry of man pleading with other man to understand each other's failure and to live together.

Miller's play thus displays the ideas of his earlier plays in greater clarity and are expressed with greater vehemence. Miller's interpretation of the myth has a strong contemporary relevance in terms of its moral and sociological meanings. An awareness of evil and of one's own limitation is essential to avoid self-righteous thoughts and actions on one's own part. It need not necessarily lead to psychological or moral guilt — the kind of guilt that plagued the puritans in *The Crucible.* At the same time, the knowledge of this shared evil should lead to a reconciliation with and understanding of other human beings. This is the message of all of Miller's later plays — *The Crucible, After The Fall, Incident At Vichy* and *The Creation,* Miller must have known that playwrights life Wilder, Connolly and Odets before him had examined the myth of Eden for searching a more contemporary and relevant meaning. That his own exploration of the myth brings up conclusions which are comparatively more humanistic and defiant, is only evident of Miller's impatience with a hypocritical world and his deep and almost religious love for his fellow man, particularly the suffering kind.

The Ride Down Mt. Mogan is the latest play to emerge from the pen of Arthur Miller who recently turned 77. Arthur Miller's autumn seems to be one of mellow fruitfulness as he turns to comedy for his latest production. *The Ride Down Mt. Morgan* is a play about bigamy that has the audience laughing loudly and often.

There is a difference between men who keep mistresses under wraps and those who insist on marrying them, as Miller's lead character Lyman does. According to Peter Lewis:

> There is a great deal of difference, too between Lyman and men such as Miller himself who have two or more wives in succession (Miller's third marriage to Inge Morath has lasted 30 years). His new play is not obviously autobiographical but the initial impact of Marilyn Monroe on his first marriage to Mary Slattery, his college sweetheart, obviously helped for the experience that made him write the play.[26]

Lyman, however, successful rich and optimistic with an insatiable appetite for life-simply marries both the women in his life. When asked by Peter Lewis, "Is Lyman meant to be despicable or interesting?" Miller replies, "To me he's both. Nowadays I'm more tolerant of my characters. I have too many things to atone for myself." In an interview with Peter Lewis, Miller goes on to say :

> He's the quintessence of the 80's, Man, the man who has everything, but there's no end to his appetite. He keeps saying he's telling the truth about himself, but in fact, he's had to conceal everything. It must be a hell of a strain! He discovers that betrayal is the first law of life, that you can either be loyal to yourself or to others, but not to both. Your only hope is to end up with the right regards.

When suggested by Peter Lewis that "Woman might take a jaundiced view of the role he has assigned them as the sex which wants life to be safe and which therefore gets deceived; Miller replies, "several women have asked me", "might not women also want to express themselves to the full by taking on more than one husband?" Their reaction to the play has been positive so far, but I'm sure there'll be kickbacks. It will probably be received with the usual mixture of bewilderment, enthusiasm and condemnation. It's too close to home to expect a conventional response. When I stand at the back of the audience, they laugh quite loudly, but you can hear the groans", he says with enthusiasm.

> I can't give people a readymade solution to something so complex. I don't give them a team to root for. You could send them out happy, but they'd only be happy until they stopped to think about it. I decided to leave it in their laps, not so much as a problem but as a life situation.

Miller comments:

> Watching a play is not like lying on a

psychiatrist's couch or sitting alone in front of the television. In the theatre you can sense the reactions of your fellow citizens alongwith your own reactions. You may learn something about yourself, but sharing it with others brings a certain relief — the feeling that — you are not alone. You're part of the human race. I think that's what theatre is about.[27]

References

1. Arthur Miller : *Introduction to the Collected Plays.* Allied Publishers, New Delhi, 1973, p. 50.
2. Arthur Miller : *On Social Plays,* p. 65.
3. *Ibid.,* p. 65.
4. Bamber Gascoigne : *Twentieth Century Drama,* Hutchinson, London, 1962, p. 180.
5. Arthur Miller : "When Life had at Least a Form", *New York Times,* Sunday, Jan. 24, 1971.
6. Quoted by Gean Gould : *Modern American Playwrights,* Chap.XII, Arthur Miller, Popular, Bombay, 1969, p. 255.
7. Robert Hogan : *Arthur Miller,* Minneapolis, Univ. of Minnesota Press, 1964, p. 32.
8. Arthur Miller : *Introduction to the Collected Plays,* Allied, 1973, pp. 47-49.
9. Robert Hogan : *Arthur Miller,* Univ. of Minnesota Press, 1964, p. 32.
10. Richard Findlater : *No Time for Tragedy, The 20th Century,* Vol. 161, No. 959, (Jan. 1957-58).
11. Arthur Gunj : "The Silence of Arthur Miller", *Drama Survey,* 3.2 (Fall 1963), p. 234.
12. Richard Findlater : "No Time for Tragedy", *The 20th Century,* Vol. 161, No. 959, (Jan. 1957), p. 60.
13. Arthur Miller : *Tragedy and the Common Man,* p. 80.
14. Bamber Gascoigne : *The Twentieth Century Drama,* London, 1962, p. 181.

15. Tenessee Williams : *The Class Menagerid,* (From aspect of Modern Drama, ed. M.N Steinberg), New York, 1960, p. 561.
16. Robert Hogan : Arthur Miller, Minnesota, 1964, p. 45.
17. Quoted by Sheila Huftel : *Arthur Miller, The Burning Glass* Citadel, New York, 1965, p. 196.
18. Robert Hogan : *Arthur Miller,* Minnesota, 1964, p. 44.
19. *Sunday Times,* 20 March, 1960.
20. Harold Clurman : Arthur Miller : *Themes and Variations,* Theatre I, New York : Hill and Wange, Inc., 1964.
21. Morris Freedom : *American Drama in Social Context,* Chap.4, "The Jewishness of Arthur Miller : His Family Epic", pp. 43, 44.
22. Leonard Mose : *Arthur Miller,* New York : Twayne, 1967, p. 140.
23. Barbara Gelb : Question : "Am I My Brother's Keeper?", *The New York Times,* Sunday, Nov. 29, 1964.
24. Eric Mottram : *Arthur Miller, The Development of a Political Dramatist in America,* (From *American Theatre,* ed. John Russell Brown and rernard Harris). p. 157.
25. Robert W. Corrigan : *Introduction : The Achievement of Arthur Miller,* (From *A Collection of Critical Essays,* ed. Robert W. Corrigan), p. 15.
26. Peter Lewis : From a Review of "The Ride Down Mt. Morgan" in *The Sunday Times,* London, Jan. 4, 1992.
27. *Ibid.*

6

The Shifting Camera

Willy: It's not what you say, It's how you say it "the words are burning.

Arthur Miller said, "A drama ought not to be looked at first and foremost from literary perspectives merely because it uses words, verbal rhythm and poetic image. These can be its most memorable parts, it is true, but they are not its inevitable accompaniments."' Miller considered the various techniques of drama as tools; for, according to him, the aim of drama is revelation of life and human motives. Hence, Miller is not rigid about the use of techniques in drama and uses the three major techniques - realistic, expressionistic and rhetorical -in this spirit. According to Miller, the playwright has a duty, a responsibility towards society which he must discharge properly. In Miller's view:

> A great drama is a great jurisprudence. Balance is all. It will evade us until we can once again see man as a whole, until authority's Sensitivity and power, justice and

> necessity are utterly face to face, until authority's justifications and rebellion's too are tracked even to those heights where the breath fails, where because the largest point of view as well as the smaller has spoken truly the rest is silence.

This is certainly a noble, lofty concept of drama. Miller once remarked that great drama would not be produced until "a play mixes 'I' with 'we' in a significantly original way. The only materials for a possible new trend in the U.S. are new insights into social and psychological machanisms; the next original interpretation of these elements, one with the other, will establish a new form. "The dramatist is hardily scared by the problem of finding a dramatic means to interrelate 'social and psychological machanisms'. In 1947, he said: "My development is toward an ever - greater examination of human nature. So many people are talking about new form." A decade later he added : "however important considerations of style and form have been to me, they are only means: tools to cry up the well-born, 'inevitable' surfaces of experience behind which swarm the living thoughts and feelings whose expression is the essential purpose of art." I The words 'regardless' and 'only' falsify the tremendous concern. Miller has shown for his 'tools' throughout his career. If his 'examination of human nature' has dwelt mainly on a single subject, his methods have certainly undergone a considerable modification. In several analyses of his own plays he illuminates those changing artistic strategies and his continous struggle with the technical questions entailed by his thematic interests.

The most penetrating and comprehensive analysis is his long Introduction to the Collected Plays. In it he indicates his involvement with three stylistic modes prevalent in modern drama -the realistic, the expressionistic and the the rhetorical. "I have stood squarely in conventional realism", he declares and an acknowledgement of a major debt to Ibsen supports the statement. Although he had gained an appreciation for the power of 'hard facts'from Dostoievsky's The Brothers Karamazov, he learned how "make the moral world . . real and evident" by observing Ibsen's "ability to forge a play upon a factual bedrock. A situation in his plays is never stated but revealed in terms of hard actions, irrevo cable deeds."[4]

While Miller embraced words, gestures and shapes of the familiar world, however, he "tried to expand (realism) with an imposition of various forms in order to speak more directly . . of what has moved me behind the visible facades of life." He expanded in two directions. From the strait of his career he wished to enrich the realistic style with an 'evaluation of life' - a conscious articulation of ethical judgement. Quite early that wish led to vexing predicament: in The Man Who Had All The Luck he realised soon after completing the work, he had not been able to avoid a rhetorical or discursive presentation of his theme. With the next plqy he determined to 'forego' any sentiments that did not arise naturally from the action. The plan in All My Sons was 'to seek cause and effect, hard action, facts, the geometry of itself unless it was literally forced out of a character's mouth." In this way miller thought he would find it possible to elicit a "relatively sharp definition of the social aspects" without resorting to the discursiveness of the earlier play.

Then Miller saw that the most significant consequences composing a character's inheritance from past decisions might be mental and emotional not physical. In Death of A Salesman, therefore, he introduced an expressionistic element to get at the passion residing behind the visible facades.

> From the theatrical viewpoint that play ... broke the bounds, I believe, of a long convention of realism. I had willingly employed expressionism but always to create a subjective truth. . I had always been attracted and repelled by the brilliance of German expressionism after World War and one aim in Salesman was to employ its quite marvellous shorthand for humane, 'felt' characterizations rather than for purposes of demonstration for which the Germans had used it. [5]

This'shorthand' reproduced the psychological immediacy of past events. The Salesman image was from the beginning absorbed with the concept that nothing in life comes 'next' but that everything exists togeter and at the same time within us.

All My sons represented a compromise between an explicit moralism and a realistic 'geometry' of causation. Death of A Selesman represented a compromise between rhetorical, realistic and expressionistic modes. After Death of A Salesman,, a preference for plays which seek causation not only in psychology but in society compelled Miller to curtail his exploration of subjective process and to return to a more objective frame of reference. In writing The Crucible he was still bemused by "a kind of interior mechanism" but he hoped to lift his study "out of the morass of subjectivism" with historical data and with evaluative declamation. "It seemed to me then" Miller writes in a 1960 Introduction to A View From The Bridge, "that the theatre was retreating into an area of psyche - sexual romanticism and this at the very moment when great events both at home and abroad cried out for recognition and analytical inspection."

Having taken a step towards a more self-aware drama with The Crucible. Miller continues in this preface, he decided to advance further into the realm ruled by "code and ideas of social and ethical importance. The fanaticism of Eddie carbone can be measured by his culture". In another essay. "On Social Plays", Miller states that by time he wrote A View From The Bridge he had abandoned his theory of 'interior' causation in favour of "bare" facts and rational commentary.

Miller's experimentation with expressionistic, realistic and rhetorical styles, then, has been conditioned by his overriding desire to declare objective truths about man in society. Miller states, "our standards of right and wrong, good taste and bad, must in some way come into either conflict or agreement with social standards. A playwright's goal should be to merge surface of experience (the objective) with cogent emotional life (the subjective) and philosophically or socially meaningful themes (the analytic) so as to make know the public significance of private engagements. Drama is skin to the other inventions of man in that it ought to help us to know more and not merely to spend our feelings. The ultimate justification for a genuine new form is the new and heightened consciousness it creates and makes possible - a consciousness of causation in the light of known but hitherto inexplicable effects."' Miller's aim as a creftman has been to "make real on stage as in life that part of man which through passion seeks awareness. There is no contradiction between the two."

Arthur Miller and Eugene O'Neill have done more than other American dramatists to relate the subjective to the objective truth. Death ofA Salesman and O'Neill's Long Day's Journey into Night are two of the finest works in the American theatre. Contrary to Miller's assertion, however, there is in his plays a contradiction between passion and awareness, between irrational impulse and rational concept. His best dialogue mirrors psychological conditions, yet he constantly returns to the formal generalization. He can skilfully manipulate emotional tension, yet he seeks aesthetic detachment. His figures act most intelligibly in a family context, yet he feels obliged to make explicit their connection with social 'environment'. Miller sees his principal subject, the drive for self - j ustification - pirmarly as an internal process activated by 'mechanisms' that repress or involutarily recall shameful memories and motives, that effect rapid transitions between taut and relaxed moods. When his carracters fervently defend egocentric attitudes, their futility evokes a genuine sense of terror and pathos that indirectly but powerfully reinforces his thesis on the necessisty for 'meaningful' accommodation in society, when, on the other hand, his characters intelligently reforms, their self - knowledge remains only a theoratical promise. The mature newman -Lawrence Newman, David Freiber, Chris keller, Biff Loman,

John Proctor, Gay Langland, Quentin, Leduc and Von Barge - appear just long enough to predicate their liberating insights.

A review of Miller's symbolic, structural and verbal techniques substantiates this conclusion. Miller has been relatively fortunate in finding apt metaphors to signify the implications of 'a gap between the private life and the social life'. Most ofhis symbolic images, it is true, are drawn along simple lines -- a carousal that conceals hatred (Focus) : a fruitful tree destroyed in its prime (All My Sons) : green leaves blotted out by the hard outlines of apartment buildings, a flute song displaced by childish nonsense from a wire recorder, a wife's praise erased by a whore's laughter (death ofA Salesman) : a dingy warehouse harbouring hopeless inmates (A Memory of Two Mondays) a herd of mustangs moving towards extinction (The Misfits): a ruined tower that memoralizes horrors committed by 'ordinary' man (After the fall) ; feathers and a broken pat guarded as if they were life itself (Incident at Vichy).

Miller's construction, if rarely flawless, is never formless. His metaphors, if sometimes obvious, are sometimes subtle. It is the dialogue that swings between extremes of brilliance and insipidity. Colloquial speech may be heard in an amazing variety of accents -- Irish, Swedish, German, Sicilian, Slavic, Barbados, Yiddish, Puritan, Brooklyn, Southwestern and Midwestern. After the Fall and Incident At Vichy, in fact, were the first works that did not make extensive use of subliterate English (except for Maggie's Newyork locutions and childish inanities, which convey a certain charm and a certain mental barrenness).Whether in historical riligion or foreign dialect, Miller's dialogue is most telling when it works by implications, not by explication.

Explicit analyses of motivation may, of course, serve a legitimate and even commendable purpose by establishing a rational perspective. Thus Biff Loman and Charley reflect on the meaning of Willy's existence; the misfits as philosophers explain the misfits as doers; Quentin during his psychoanalysis contemplates Quentin before, Leduc and Von Berg answer the question puzzling the other prisoners. At other times, trivial homespun talk, unable to bridge the 'gap separating passion from formal communication, dumbly marks unspeakable humiliation, wrath or sorrow; then Miller's writing attains its greatest power. Joe Keller's bluff words resound with increasing apprehension. "Because it's good money there's nothing wrong with that money". "What have I got to hide ? What the hell is the matter with you?.

In a similar way, Willy Loman's commonplace constructions define uncommon motives. "He won't Starve. None of them starve." Charley advises concerning Biff, 'forget about him'. Willy answers with the poignantly simple sentence, "then what have I got to remember T' The'Crucible like Death of A Salesman contains some self-conscious oratory. The puritan dialect may sound archaic and formal to a present-day audience, but it can be as impressive in its monosyllabic directness as contemporary English. "It were a fearsome man". Rebecca eulogizes over one of the witch-hunt victims. "Spite only keeps me silent". Proctor says; "it is hard to give the lie to gogs."

Miller favours a logical structure, an organic whole, in plays. Insisting on "the organic necessity". Miller remarks:

> 'That a play is written prosaically does not make it a realistic play, and that the speech is heightened and intensified by imagery does not set it to one side of realism necessarily. The underlying poem of a play I take to be the organic necessity of its parts. I find in the arbitrary not poetry but indulgence.'

Miller's sense of relatedness is evident in his plays. His parts may be episodic in character, but his wholes are usually effective and unforgettable.

Expressionism is the most dominant technique of the 20th century and except for this, drama should have remained a dead art. Still even today to be expressionistic is to be 'modern'.

In fact, most of the American expressionist playwrights started as realists. Strindberg wrote realistic plays before he embarked upon symbolist and expressionist mode of writing, O'Neill began as a realist, wrote some of his best expressionist plays of the century and then went back to realism. Elmer rice, Arthur Miller, Tennesses Williams, Thronton Wilder and a number of other playwrights did the same. Among the American playwrights only O'Neill, Miller and Williams could successfully fuse realism into their expressionistic technique. Acording to Dr. V Rama Murthy

> Expressionism is not entirely a new art. One may find its origin in some

> of the plays of Shakespeare, in Everyman and in the Greek Tragedies. The witches in Shakespeare's Macbeth. lo. the wandering woman in Aeschylus's prometheus Bound, characters like Good Deeds and Fellowship in Everyman are forerunners of expressionistic characters!

There was an attempt at expressionistic dramatization even in the medieval plays. In these plays a simultaneous presentation of the hell, paradise, the garden of Eden and the place where Christ died was made. Such a simulaniety gave a symbolic or allegorical meaning to the events presented. The sins and sufferings mentioned in the Bible were also reenacted in contemporary constumes and language.

In the realistic theatre the emphasis was laid'on physical realism. A drawing room with familiar furniture, commonsense dialogue and ordinary converasation formed parts of the play. But the expressionist drama is based on psychological realism. To the expressionist dramatist reality is something that man daily cheats himself into believing. To him realism is a mere illusion which preserves only the appearance of reality and not a revealing image of it and therefore, he tries to throw some special light on reality by shifting his dramatic focus from the external to the interior. He creates various symbols and symbolic devices to project the inner world of the play on the stage. Expressionism, in the words of Elmer Rice,

> "attempts to go beyond more representation and to arrive at

> interpretation. The author attempts no sc much to depict events faithfully as to convey to the spectator what seems to be their inner significance. To achieve this end, the dramatist often finds it expedient to depart entirely from objective reality and to employ symbols, condensations and a dozen devices which to the conservative must seem arbitrarily fantastic."

The expressionist dramatist does not maintain anypretense of showing life as we ordinarily see it. He concentrates directly on what goes on in the mind of the hero without any concern for naturalistic portrayal of his suffering. The setting is also made purposefully of unfamiliar pieces.

Sometimes it is so unfamiliar that it may appear to be too theatrical. On the stage we are made to see so many weird and fantastic images of experience. The characters themselves become mental images explaining a mental process.

So many of the old conventions have been used by the expressionist dramatist in different ways. In the old plays the chorus or the confidant served the purpose of a commentator. The hero would reveal his innermost thoughts to them and elicit their comments. Sometimes the 'aside' helped the hero reveal his innermost motives. In the Greek and the Roman theatres marks were used as a way of pressenting the inner working of the character's mind. In the expressionist plays these devices varied according to the theme and situation and the whims of the playwright. A dramatist like O'Neill used masks most liberally. Arthur Miller used the 'flashback' in his Death of A Salesman. Willy Loman, the protagonist recalls to his mind the past events in his life and they are thus featured simultaneously on the stage.

In most of these plays the set itself serves as an allegorical form for the substance of the play. In Georg Kaiser's From Mom to Midnight, the earliest expressionist play, life is presented as a sevenday bicycle race. While the race is on, the people keep on hoping that there will be a serious acident. In an image like this Kaiser finds a dramatic equivalent for the futile competition in which man's life is wasted.

Elmer Rice's The Adding Machine is a similar play in which the principal character is a dull accountant whose name is Mr. Zero. He murders his employer and for this he is made to work in the Elysian field on an adding machine. He works at it till he becomes a soulless slave of it. This play is also a comment on the machanization of man. In Thronton wilder's The Skin of Our Teeth a dinosaur and a mammoth are brought on the stage to indicate the pre-historic times of man. The playwright tries to present the story of the survival of man from pre-historic times to modem times. It was, however, strindberg who wrote the most influential expressionist plays. In his A Dream Play a poet envisions Indra's daughter coming down from heaven and suffering with all humanity. She finds the world to be a "pestilent congregation of vapours" with its miseries far exceeding its pleasures. There are contradictions everywhere and these are resolved in death which, according to Strindberg, is the only clean and pure state.

Since Strindberg, expressionism has been and is still continuing to be the driving force behind a whole generation of artists. It has instilled new life into art, music and literature. Strindberg, the earliest exponent of expressionism, felt that no formal story, linear or the Aristotelian plot could contain the ambiguity of human nature. So from the linear he turned to the circular form. A drama like A Dream Play consists of montage of scenes which do not progress and which are meaningful not in sequence but in suspense. In Death of A Salesman much of the plot moves back and forth from a central situation. In Camino Real the events are projected on the stage almost simultaneously instead of sequentially.

All these plays exist in a timeless world, in the interior, in recollection or dream or fantasy. "Such plays". Marvin Rosenbnerg says",

> "presents a discontinuous psychic activity. They translate the restless intensity of inner light into busy, loaded symbolic action. Many perspectives of the same perception are brought together; many intense momentary chorded expressions poise side by side in tension; and the dynamic'context conveys a sense of the ever dissolving jestalts of existence."[10]

Only three plays in our times have achieved the perfectintegration of expressionism and realism. They are : O'Neill's The Hairy Ape. Tennessee Williams's The Glass Menagerie and Arthur Miller's Death of a Salesman. In all these plays, expression, expressionism has been meaning fully and fruitfully employed. Their authors certainly go farther than Ibsen but not as far as Kaiser or Toller. They have a logical consistency and an original structure that other plays lack. They are unsurpassed in their construction and power of situation. In all of them there is a harmonious blending of realism with non-realistic or expressionistic stylization.

Arthur Miller exposes the basic malaise of society, which is responsible for the nerve-racking tensions and worries of modern man. He views the individual not in isolation as Williams does but in relation to the environments. Though his moral earnestness sometimes sounds puritanical and oldfashioned the powerful dramatic element in his plays makes them interesting as plays.

The resurgence of American drama is chiefly due to the integrity of such artists as O'Neill, Miller and Williams. They have always tried to remain loyal to their artistic vision and assert their primacy over the producer, the director or even the audience. Turning over the manuscript of Death of A Salesman to producers with a very complex plot involving simultaneous presentation of the scenes from the past, the present and the future of hero's life. Arthur Miller said:

"I don't know how this can be solved; the designer of this production must find a very simple solution."

The house in Death of A Salesman is expressionistic. There are towering, angular slopes behind the house surrounding it on all sides. There is an 'angry glow of orange' and around the house. There is, however, a blue light falling on the house.

Willy is cramped in between these buildings with the high aspiration of a low man. The setting of Death of A Salesman also was done in the Brechtian epic manner. A gravestone with a wreath of flowers on a bare stage will do for the graveyard scene.

The music of the flute recurs throughout the play connecting his memories with his father who used to travel with a wagon full of flutes. The leaves appear and disappear indicating the stage of his mind. No curtain is used. Brooklyn, Boston and New York are cohered without moving the scenery. The house, trees and leaves and the tape-recorder, the werird woman's daughter, the sowing of seeds by Willy are all symbolic. The motorcar is the symbol of middle - class aspiration.

His sowing of seeds indicates his strong desire to have something refreshing in that dreariness. But he has no place for it and his surroundings are so hostile to it that nothing ever grows there. The weird woman constantly reminds him of his past and makes him feel guilty. This shows that Willy is sensitive and is capable of penitence. The expressionistic form and the realistic theme are so well blended that one heightens the effect of the other. The psychological reality becomes the physical reality.

The baring of the consciousness of Willy brings to light the motif of quest for values and identity in the play. Willy lacks the vision to look beyond the meaingless chores and attidudes of a mechanistic civilization of which he is a conforming member. Thus he sustains the illusions throughout his life and is not disillusioned even when he commits suicide. willy implicitly seeks his identity in different, ways -sometimes in Ben, sometimes in Biff and Happy. However, his efforts do not lead him anywhere because of his lack of awareness of reality. When Biff tries to tell him that he is nothing, he reacts sharply and says that he is still Willy Loman. The illusions of Willy are not shattered because they are intermingled with his 'ideals' and he cannot even bear to think of the shattering of his false ideals which he has tried unsuccessfully to achieve all through his life.

Miller's ideas and his technique are best illustrated in Death of A Salesman. The play exhibits all the most characteristic traits, in their plainest, most emphatic form. Plainness is achieved because Miller makes a principle out of his usual vagueness.The principle is Expressionism. The vague, typical hero becomes the embodiment of typicality. Willy, the low man, who carries his status in his name. His friends Charley and Bernard -- the only other family we see -- have no last name at all, and neither does Willy's employer. Further -more, the salesman is, as we have observed, the most representative member of our commercial society; in a sense, when the salesman dies, this society dies. Every strand of evidence, in and out of the play, points to the symbolic reading of the salesman's role. Replying to the many salesmen who thought they saw their own story writ large in the play. Miller has insisted : 'I have and had not the slightest interest in the selling profession.' The mystery of the salesman's product is preserved for symbolic reasons. Miller tantalizes us with references to stores in Boston and to Willy's eye for color, but, in response to questions, he invariably answered that the product Willy was selling was himself. Preserving the mystery keeps Willy the archetypal salesman of our time.

Willy is much more emphatically a representative figure, an American Everyman, than any of Miller's other characters. Accordingly, his problems are much less personal dilemmas than they are public issues. Willy is a useful instrument for Miller's social criticism. This quality of his is the first trait by which we identify this play as an example of Expressionism. Certainly this concern with large social issues is the key to Miller's definition of Expressionism in his Harvard lecture:

> It is a form ... which manifestly seeks to dramatize the conflict of either social, religious or moral forces per se. "

In one of his articles, Miller finds that the Greeks and the Expressionists are alike in their effort "to present the hidden forces."

Miller's first successful play, All My Sons shows signs of the most careful, almost academic, planning. It is an Ibsen - like story of guilt from the past permeating anddestroying the present. Joe Keller is an industrialist. His double crime is that during the war he sold the government's batch of faulty cylinder heads, which caused the death of twenty- one pilots and later laid all the blame on his innocnt manager, Deever. Deever is still in gaol, but Keller, although temporarily ruined, has again become a prosperous citizen. The characters are carefully graded to draw every last irony and implication from the story.

Arthur Miller is claimed by many to have given a new form and a substance to American Drama.

Miller consolidated his position in the theatre not only as a first-rate craftsman but also as a writer who is not afraid to tackle contemporary problems. In fact, his main preoccupation in all his plays is with individual and social morality. In both All My Sons and Death of A Salesman the personal tragedy springs directly from the protagonist's fidelity to values with the welfare of mankind. Both Joe Keller and Willy Loman realise too late that they have bartered their soul for a mess of freeenterprise pottage. Their central obsession is that their own happiness and that of those they love is dependent, first and foremost, on their success in life or business depends on appearances. They fail to make any connection between their private and public roles. They commit suicide because by adhering to social morality they have aff-ronted moral decency.

Though all Miller's plays are grounded in the environment with which he is most familiar, they have been able to strike responsive chords in people everywhere, testifying to their essential universal quality. His themes are, timeless and temely. They are in the tradition of Greek tragedy. A keen intellectual who has painstakingly crafted and evaluated his work. Miller is concerned with creating tragic drama of the Greek calibre in the age of the common man. He has consciously sought to aply classical and universal concepts to the drama of the 20th century.

In All My Sons, Miller tries to create tragic drama of the Greek genre in an age of the common man. His tragic characters are not at all exceptional, outstanding or bizarre. They are common decent men and the tragic flaw exists more strongly in their milieu than in them. They become, in a sense, the victims of external circumstances. Thus All My sons is a dexterously constructed Greek-type tragedy in a modem setting. Joe's hamartia or lack of insight about what constitutes personal ethics triggers the tragedy. His tragedy succeeds in effecting Cathararsis in us.

As in Oedipus Rex or Ghosts, the real plot of All My Sons emerges from the present action like a ghost from the past. It comes to dominate that action and to be the centre of the play. This plot from the past, even in the beginning of the play, is constantly intruded. We are constantly remained of Joe's trial and Larry's death. such a technique may seem at first to slow the pace, until we see that it is revealing the real action. When such a parallel plot is well handled, there is a suspenseful tension as the relationship between past and present becomes ever-clearer.

Like Ibsen's social plays, Miller's play is economical. All of his characters, even the minor ones, have an integral relation to the theme. No characters are introduced merely to illustrate or to facilitate the mechanics of the plot. Such economy emphasizes the play's closeness to traditional austere tragedy. This is a family tragedy; the father is a man of some importance who falls from power to ignominy. The lives of his entire family are blighted by his crime. There is even in the play a hint of fate inexorably guiding the destinies of the characters. It is a ghost from the past, the deadson, whose words precipitate the tragic climax. In one of the minor characters who is preparing a horoscope of the dead son, the play even has a prophet that last fact suggests the distance between the austere stylized tragedy of Sophocles and Racine and the austere, realistic tragedy of Ibsen and Miller.

The advance on The Man Who Had All the Luck is evident in this play both in theme and technique. The confident certainty of dramatic movement in this play seems deliberately and successfully counterpoised against the loss of certainty that is the play's main theme. The keynote of the play is its questioning. Dialogue in the theatre is regularly carried on in terms of questions and answers, but in All My Sons the questions are in effect dialogue stoppers. The dramatic power resides in the sort of questions asked and in the inability of the characters to answer them. Particularly prominent in the last act and in the exchanges between Jo ' e and the powerful climax to the second act in Chris's agonized reiteration of such questions as "where do you live, where have you come from ? ... What must I do Jesus God, what must I do T' Nothing brings out joe Keller's bewildered isolation better than this exchange with his wife:

Keller : May be I ought to talk to Ann ?

Mother : Don't aske me, Joe;

Keller : (almost an outburst) : Then who do I ask ? But I don't think she'll do anything about it.

Mother : You are asking me again.

Keller : I'm askin' you. Whom am 1, a stranger ? I thought I had a family here. What happened to my family?

Mother : You've got a family I'm simply telling you that I have no strength to think any more.....

Keller : Then what do I do ? Tell me, talk to me, what do I do T'

The decade of the fifties saw a steady growth of Miller's dramatic art. During this period he wrote The Crucible. A Memory of Two Mondays and A View from The Bridge. These plays show his growing hold on the materials of art.

The subject of The Crucible - the Salem witch-trials of 1692, was distractingly applicable to what has been called the witch hunts of 1950's. The Crucible is a strong play and its conclusion has much of the force of tragedy. It has not the permeating compassion ofDeath of A Salesman, but there is more dramatic power to John Proctor's death than there was to Willy's. It is a harder hitting play, and its impact stems from Proctor's death being really a triumph. Willy Loman's death was a failure, and his suicide only a gesture of defeat. Him one can pity.

The Crucible is really a more dramatic play than Death of A Salesman. The plots of Death of A Salesman are not the centre of the play, but in The Crucible the action is the play's very basis, its consuming centre. One watches Death of A Salesman to discover what a man is like, but one watches The Crucible to disvoer what a man does. In the life of John Proctor, one single action is decisive, dominating and totally pertinent and this action, this moment of decision and commitment, is that climax toward which every incident in the play tends. Death of A Salesman is not traditionally dramatic, at least in the Aristotelian sense that the centre of a drama is an action. The Crucible is so dramatic and the centrality of its plot explains its greater strength. That strength is alsoexplained by the clarity with which the theme of The Crucible emerges from its plot. The theme of Death of A Salesman does not emerge so much from its story as from its illustration and exposition. For that reason it is necessary for Linda and Charley in their laments to explain the meaning of willy's life and actually Linda is still explaining what the play means in the last scene. The Crucible requires no such exposition, for the play's meaning has been acutely dramatized.

Technically the play is not as interesting as Death of A Salesman or as tightly structured as All My Sons. Its structure is, however, appropriate for the retelling of the witch hunt story and for the revelation to Proctor of the need for commitment. Its language is not as lyrically avocative as that of Death of A Salesman, but it does not need to be. In Death of A Salesman language had to be substitute for plot; here it can be unobtrusively subservient. Actually the dialogue of the play is a considerable accomplishment. It suggests the flavour of seventeenth-century speech without becoming distractingly archaic and without sacrificing simplicity, strength or suppleness.

Because of its concentration on moral issues and on the conflict between good and evil in the context of a christian society. The Crucible is linked to the 'morality plays' popular in medieval England. In the most famous of these, Everyman, the central character's name shows what he symbolises, and the other characters are similarly named aft er the abstract qualities that they personify. The story is plainly allegorical. Everyman is visited by Death who tells him to prepare for a joumey, and he asks fellowship, Kinsmen and Goods to accompany him, only to find that Good-deeds alone can go with him.

It could be said that, in The Crucible, Abigail represents Lust, Putnam is Greed, Parris is credulity, Hale is Good Intentions, Elizabeth is loyality and so on. However, it would be an oversimplification to say that the charactyers in The Crucible, like those in the moralities, are symbols rather than people, that Miller's interest in them extends only to what he can make them represent. According to Dennis Welland, "They must be considered strictly as the fictitious creations of a dramatist and quite independent of their historical counterparts."[12]

The play is a parable only to the extent that it shows that the Salem trials throw light on persecutions and pogroms in totallitarian regimes and even in democratic societies when they are seized by panic. But surely, the characters in The Crucible are not mere mouthpieces of various points of view. Abigail, Parris, the Proctors and Hale are certainly lifelike characters. The dry bones of history get infused with life. The records of the trial contain statements and confessions, questions and answers. But in the play, the accusers, the accused, the judges and the community in which they live become real.

The play derives its value from the fact that its theme is not merely of historical or academic interest. It is of significance at all times and is of particular concern to us today.

A Memory of Two Mondays, is Miller's simplest play and appears to be his most purely autobiographical. The play is a considerable achievement. Tragi-comedy requires that the stories of a number of people be told. It requires that not merely one mood but various conflicting ones be evoked. It usually requires irony and it oftem uses lyricism and song. These qualities are all present in Miller's play, and it is remarkable that he was able to pack so much so effectively. In a way, it is like trying to pack The Plough and the Stars into one act and succeeding. This is amoving, technically adroit and beautiful job, one of the rare instances of a one-act tragi-comedy.

Miller's descent from the austere tragic form is nowhere more evident than in the first version ofA View From the Bridge. The play seems an attempt to utilize the austere technique of Sophocles in a modern setting, just as Maxwell Anderson's Winterset was an atempt to do the same thing with the manner of Shakespeare.

The play is strongly effective on the stage, yet, except in the broadest sense as a story of a man driven by a secret passion. It probably has a lesser relevance than do the stories of Joe Keller or Willy Loman. Like Willy, Eddie does not fully understand or at least admit the force that is destroying him, and, like John Proctor, Eddie is ultimately concerned with waving his name. At the climactic moments of both The Crucible and AView From The Bridge, the protagonist is destroyed by his need to secure a place in society. In all of Miller's plays up to this time, morality is established by the society. In Death of A Salesman and The Crucible, the morality is false; in All My Sons and AView From the Bridge, it is valid. Up to this last play. Miller still saw the establishment of a social morality as the way out of the impasse of studies of individual distintegration which formed the subjects of the bulk of serious drama and fiction in modern times.

After the Fall is the most introspective play that Miller has written. It has assumed the form of an interior dialogue, a progress in self-discovery accomplished without a psychiatrist. "This play", Miller wrote in the Foreword,

> "is a trial; the trial of a man by his
>
> own conscience, his own values, his own
>
> deeds. The listener (an unseen character
>
> addressed by Quentin, the progagonist)
>
> who to some will be a psychoanalyst, to
>
> others God, is Quentin himself turned
>
> at the stage of the abyss to look at his
>
> nature and his time."[13]

After the Fall is Miller's most intellectually probing play, and Quentin is a central character too complicated to be summed up by simple reactions of love and pity. The play tells what happens to a man after the loss of intellectual innocence, after his fall. Simple views of morality have failed Quentin, and he has lost his innocence not only as individual but as a member of the family and a member of society as well. As an individual, he has seen the wreckage of two marriages. He has seen the failure of love both in his own family and among his friends.

both in his own country and in the world-almost every person in this play betrays love.

Technically, the play is a brilliant accomplishment. In it Miller solves his perennial problem of how to retain sufficient real psychology and a full feel of the real world and at the same time to attain a free flow of time and to probe more deeply into a man's mind than conventional realism allows. This play manages all of these matters without falling into the pitfalls of extreme expressionism of the Theatre of the Absured. The play is told to an invisible narrator who might be, as Miller observes, Quentin's analyst or God, but who really is Quentin himself. The play is an examination of conscience, and it takes place -- to use the title which Miller discarded for Death of A Salesman -- 'Inside His Mind'.

Incident At Vichy is a play in which nine men and a boy are picked off as suspected Jews, are interrogated and humiliated. There is a communist worker for whom the meaning of suffering is not personal but historical, a matter of 'the economic and political forces.' 'He has faith in the future and the future is socialist'. There is an anarchist who believes that only god knows what things mean.

There are others ... a businessman who is confident that he will be released, an aristocrat who thinks that Nazism is not an ideology but 'an outburst of vulgarity', and an actor who believes that one plays a role to suit the circumstances. The play seems to depict a total disenchantment with various systems, ideologies and even love. Every thing seems to be a struggle between ciphers. Men are killers and they have an irrational murderous nature. Life is possible, Miller seems to feel, only after the recognition of the individual's part in the evil he sees and abhors. Eric Mottram points out that :

> "Miller is caught between a belief in a fixed 'human nature' and desire to see it change. His anguish is distressing and devitalizing in its futility. The majority of the world strives forward for peaceful freedom from power situations and their dehumanizing violence, whether in peace or war. Miller, with honesty and persistence and degree of dramatic skill, remains fixed in a hell which he maintains cannot be outdated."[14]

In The Price. Miller once again goes back to the conventional realistic form and the typical situation of two sons trying to examine their relationship with their father. It is Miller's concern with life's balance of payments that he explores in his play, The Price. What Miller is challenginng is the whole idea of moral debt based on 'Price'. For whenever people try to relate to each other in terms of the price to be paid, they will always get less than they bargained for; the price is never enough. Both Walter and Victor have been wrong; in life there can be bo question of success or failure, or 'I gave more than you'. This is the significance of Gregory Solemon, the used furniture dealer who has come to purchase the junk heap of their past.

Solomon, wisely enough, thinks that it is silly for the brothers to worry about the price, because it will always be fair. Whether the final price offered for the furniture is $ 2.5 0 or $ 25,000 really does not matter since, as he says, the price of the used furniture of our lives is only viewpoint, and we can never deal with life's real issues in terms of quid pro quo. In addition to pointing up the fact that paying the price is finally irrelevant -- both the brothers have paid a heavy price, but so what ? Solomon's presence serves two other important functions. After dominating a good share of first act, the old man is shunted to the bedroom shortly after Walter arrives on the scene, and the second act is primarily devoted to the conflict of the brothers. But Solomon does not disappear altogether and each of his entrances is significant. In effect, he serves to keep the brothers honest; his interruptions deter them from arriving at false or illusory solutions.

In Arthur Miller's Plays, the quest becomes a search for identity, which coupled with a sense of guilt results in the recognition that the dream of perfection is hopeless. The Misfits, a short story that later became a screenplay, shows the hopelessness of the dream in the significant metaphor of the misfit. The three cow boys, although they are running from unfortunate pasts, are rootless because of their contempt for steady and settled life. The irony of these outcasts is that whereas open spaces become their ideal of freedom, they trap wild horses from open spaces to sell them for food. Their exertions to bring about the 'fall' of the Stallion symbolize the force of society to bring them (the cowboys) to their knees. They do to the horses what society does to them. Because the horses represent what cow boys seek, their aggresiveness turns back on themselves so that their dream of freedom becomes selfdestructive. The last scene of the wild horses leaping in the air and 'striking at the sky' in their captivity, underlines the paradox of the cowboys'lives. That is, their defiance of, and their dependence on society. But the dream of freedom will continue in exploring other regions till the wild horses are taken. Then, perhaps, the dream will die or be transferred to another hopeless quest.

References

1. Arthur Miller : "Introduction", Collected Plays, Allied Publishers, New Delhi, 1972, p. 9.
2. *Ibid.,* p. 11.
3. *Ibid.,* p. 13.
4. *Ibid.,* p. 21.
5. *Ibid.,* p. 27.
6. *Ibid.* p. 21.
7. *Ibid.,* p. $.
8. Dr. V. Rama Murthy, American Expressionistic Dramal Doaba House, Delhi, 1970, p. 3.
9. Elmer Rice : The Living Theatre, William Heinemann Ltd., London, 1959, p. 124.
10. Marvin Rosenberg: A Metapher for Dramatic form included in directions in Modern Theatre by John Gassner, Rolt, Rinehart and Winston, Inc., New York,, *1966, P. 3 5 1.*
11. Arthur Miller: "The Family in Modern, Drama" Atlantic Monthly, April, *19 5 6, P. 14*
12. Dennis Welland: Aurthur Miller, Oliver & Boyd. Edi *1959, P. 117*
13. Arthur Miller : Foreword to After the Fall, Viking, *1964, P.* B.
14. Eric Mottram : The Development of a Political Dramatist, American Theatre, Stratford Upon-Avon Studies, *1967, P. 161.*

7

The Allegory of Quest

(Meaning and Evaluation)

Linda : A Small man can be just a as exhausted as a greatman.

The *fin mot* of modern western drama is the motive of quest, a search for a meaningful stance against the panorama of immense anarchy and futility. Arthur Miller's theatre is a part of this mainstream as his plays explore the dilemma of protagonists who are lost *en route* in the labyrinth of life and reality. Modern theatre is an allegory of quest; a theatre of purpose, creating the protagonist in search, his Everyman in whom he dramatizes the struggle of contemporary man with the forces of his age. In fact, a careful explication of Miller's dramatic tenor reveals the moral concern of the playwright. Like Williams, Miller is deeply concerned with the ethical function of theatre, like Ibsen, Strindberg, Chekhov, Tolstoy, Shaw and O'Neill, Miller has used the theatre as a platform for interpreting the human dilemma in the twentieth century as a crisis of conscience, as a growing conflict within human consciousness. For Miller as for Dante the essential purpose of the theatre is to show man the root of his suffering and its function to play out humanity's crisis to give its tortured consciousness a concrete shape.

Arthur Miller made his professional appearance as a full-fledged playwright with *The Man Who had All the Luck.* The main quality of the play is its stress on moral responsibility. The relationship between Amos and Pat Beeves in this play is an embryonic form of the father-son antagonism that was to occupy the two later plays. *All My Sons* and *Death of a Salesman.* In all three works, a well-meaning father forfeits the respect of his son by forcing him to accept his own standard of success. Pat Beeves tries to mould Amos into a base-ball pitcher. On the whole the play reads like a moral fable dealing with the themes of money, morality and father-son relationship. *An Enemy of the People* went right to the heart of the question of an individual's will and ability to challenge the assumptions of his own society. Indeed, one of the play's characters precisely raises the question "without power, what good is the truth," Again he dramatises the plight of a man who must decide whether his responsibility is owed first to his family or to the wider world whether the truth, indeed, is an absolute necessity.

All My Sons is, according to Miller, a play written for a prophetic theatre. By a prophetic theatre he implied something:

> "seriously meant for people of common sense, and relevant to both their domestic lives and their daily work and an experience which widens their

> awareness of connection ... the filaments to the past and the future which lie concealed in life."[1]

In fact, "*All My Sons* is a realistic play illustrating the theme that a man must recognise his ethical responsibility to the world outside his home as well as in his own home."[2] A father's sin of producing shoddy war material for a profit results in the death of twenty-one American pilots and in the alienation of his family. Joe Keller, the protagonist, is faced with a choice between an aesthetic life in pursuit of heteronomous pleasure and an ethical life, which is attained by a self-determined acceptance of guilt and duty. In *All My Sons,* the hero Joe Keller represents this consciousness. His journey from self- to non-self makes the end of the quest. *All My Sons* is the author's contention that no individual's action can be self-contained, nor even within the campus of the family : Miller who wrote *All My Sons* with human understanding but moral sinew as well as taut dramaturgy summarized his theme as

> "the responsibility of man to society or the responsibility of man to his actions as a recognition of his ethical responsibility to the world and outside his home as well as in his own home."[3]

Death of a Salesman is concerned with the problems of the individual in fulfilling himself as a human being in modern society. The play indirectly makes a plea for a return to genuine friendship, to respect for the individual and to finding some way of satisfying man's needs in work that modern society with its synthetic, mass-produced, machine-made goods is ignoring. We may dislike Willy's ways of trying to succeed, but we should respond to his desire for respect for himself and his family.

> Miller's recurring themes are the relationship of the individual to society and the personal responsibility that the individual owes to society and the society failing the individual.[4]

'Evil' is the outcome of the conflict between the social pressure and the individual's will to succeed. *The Man Who had All the Luck* exposes a man's struggle in success. In *All My Sons* Keller says: "I am his father and he's my son, and if there's something bigger than that, I'll put a bullet in my head." Miller tries to earn the sympathy of the audience for him and makes him a martyr to a false ethic of family and business sentimentality. His heroes are imperfect creatures, mean, boastful and selfish. By making them martyrs at the end, Miller seems to have abused his artistic powers. But he says that he tries to "unveil a truth, already known but not recognised. The theatre can help to make man more human ... that is, alone."[5]

Arthur Miller's *The Crucible* makes use of history as allegory to depict a contemporary situation. The story of *The Crucible* takes us back to the America of the seventeenth century when there was widespread fear of witchcraft. Under the dominance of the church several innocent persons were tortured and put to death. The hero of the play John Proctor is also falsely accused of witchcraft and there is a trial during which much of the evil and hypocrisy of the orthodox society are exposed. At the end when John Proctor is given a chance to save his life by signing a confession of his complicity, he chooses to be sentenced to death rather than implicate his name in a falsehood that will wipe out his identity. As is well known, tragedy portrays undeserved suffering without leaving us desperate or dejected or obsessed with a feeling of the worthlessness of life. The hero fails or dies, but in his failure or death there is a triumph. Pity and terror are evoked, but at the end there is 'calm of mind, all passion spent'. Tragedy shows us life in depth, provokes reactions about the significance and value of life and affects us to the roots of our being. Judged by these criteria, *The Crucible* must be regarded as a fairly successful tragedy. Proctor's decision to die rather than buy life with a false confession is the catastrophe of the play. And the decision is preceded by agonizing soul-searching. Till the very end, he has a chance to save himself. His choosing to die answers the question, "What shall it profit a man if he shall gain the world and lose his own soul?" His suffering and death are undeserved and he demonstrates the strength of a moral conviction that can defy death.

A Memory of Two Mondays is about many things. The play is a moral romance. It expresses a preoccupation with the facts that everything we do in this fragmented world is so quickly wiped away and the goals when achieved, are so disappointing. The relationship between a man's identity and the image that society demands of him is a rearing theme of Miller's plays. In *A Memory of Two Mondays,* we come across the crisis of an individual acceptance and rejection of an image that is the product of his society's values and prejudices. *A Memory of Two Mondays* has a universal appeal. Miller remarks, "It was meant to be a leaf of bread for people when I thought they were getting sick with cake."[6] John

Gassner rightly finds *A Memory of Two Mondays*, "a sensitive and admirably genre piece."[7] Robert Hogan also finds Miller "able to pack so much in so effectively." For Hogan

> "in a way it is like trying to pack the 'Plough and the Stara' into one act and succeeding. This is a moving, technically adroit and beautiful job, one of the rare, instances of a one-act tragi-comedy."[8]

The protagonist of *A View From the Bridge* acts in a specific, social milieu that conditions his sense of guilt and his sense of dignity. *A View From the Bridge* is, in fact, an intriguing psychological study that shows the self-destructiveness of an inflexible, passionate individual. As such, the play resembles *All My Sons, Death of a Salesman* and *The Crucible.* Again, however, Miller hoped to enlarge his scope beyond that of psychological analysis. He worked, toward this end with Alfieri's commentary and with the Vendetta between Eddie and Marco. As narrator, Alfieri, a contemporary substitute for the Greek chorus, establishes a rhetorical contrast with Eddie much greater than that Chris and Joe Keller.

Death of a Salesman was written "in a mood of friendly partnership with the audience", *A Memory of Two Mondays* with personal love. "Miller creates in *A View From the Bridge* a modern tragic drama out of a story heard years before", with an attitude "of passionate detachment."[9] In *A View From the Bridge* Arthur Miller deals directly and heroically with the problem of betrayal. This is a play about an informer and all else is secondary to that fact and just as in *The Crucible,* Miller sought for and found a classic

American setting, so here does he take out an ancient Italian and human condition. The play is family representative.

After the Fall is the most introspective play that Miller has written. It has assumed the form of an interior dialogue, a progress in self-discovery accomplished without a psychiatrist. "This play", Miller wrote in the Foreword, "is a trial; the trial of a man by his own conscience, his own values, his own deeds. The Listener (an unseen character addressed by Quentin, the protagonist) who to some will be psychoanalyst, to others God, is Quentin himself turned at the edge of the abyss to look at his experience, his nature and his time." In *After the Fall,* Miller dealt with his local themes of faith and meaning within the confused national and personal life of America and dealt with them without obstructions which might call for a rethinking of the great society. It is the first of Miller's plays where the main emphasis is almost personal. It is also the first of Miller's plays where the largest part of the action concerns itself with martial relationships. *After the Fall* is Miller's self-revelation and a trenchant comment on the nature of profit, necessity and American moral behaviour in mid-century-

a re-working of *The Crucible* in contemporary terms into which he worked his own American confusions of public and private life.

In *Incident at Vichy* Miller closes in on the crucial question of guilt and responsibility in a dialogue between a Jewish doctor and an Austrian Prince, detained by mistake, who believes himself to be a moral man. The doctor wrings from the prince an admission that he has "somewhere hidden in his mind, a hatred for the Jews" and that each man has his Jews — "including the Jews."[10] *Incident at Vichy* repeates Miller's usual theme of self-knowledge under the pressure of forces both temperamental and environmental. In *All My Sons,* the awareness of evil is blinded by Joe Keller's passionate attachment to his loyalty to the family. The narrow walls of loyalty to the family suddenly collapse under the weight of his direct responsibility for the death of all the victims of the air-crash. The self-awareness of evil impels Joe Keller to commit suicide. The suicide of Willy Loman is the expression of tragic helplessness in Willy which transcends the limitation of material success. John Proctor's heroic resistance to the social evil becomes convincing only in the historical context of the play. The agonising awareness of evil in Quentin in *After the Fall,* in spite of his depth in probing is too passive to save Maggie. The freshness of Incident at Vichy consists in the play's capacity to transform the sense of guilt into responsibility. According to Howard Taubman, 'Miller has written a moving play, one of the most important plays of our time .... *Incident at Vichy* is a drama of towering moral passion ... it is a thundering cry of anguish that might issue from the heart of a prophet'.

The whole tenor of Miller's plays reveals the truth that his theatre is a quest, a philosophical exploration into modern human predicament. Artaud affirms that a play "is willy-willy metaphysical and it is just its metaphysical bearing, I should say the intensity of its metaphysical effort, that comprises its essential worth."[11] There is another variant of Ionesco famous comment in which the distinction between art and philosophy is sought to be obliterated:

> "since the artist comprehends reality directly, he is a true philosopher. And it is the broadness, the depth, the sharpness of philosophical vision, his living philosophy which determine his greatness."[12]

References

1. "Preface", *Collected Plays of Arthur Miller.* Viking Press, New York, 1957, p. 306.
2. Carff B. Wilson : *Three Hundred Years of American Drama and Theatre, Playwrights between two world wars,*Chap. 19, University of California, Berkley, 1959, p. 446.
3. John Gassner (ed.): *From Henrik Ibsen to Eugene Ionesco,* Third College Edition, New York : The Dryden Press, 1952, p.1061.
4. Dr. Murthy V. Rama : *American Expressionistic Drama,* Doaba House, Delhi, p. 82.
5. Arthur Miller : Preface to *Collected Plays,* New York, Viking Press, 1957, p. 306.
6. Arthur Miller : "When Life had at Least a Form", New York Times, Sunday, Jan. 24, 1971.
7. Quoted by Gean Gould : *Modern American Playwrights,* Chap. XII, Arthur Miller, Popular, Bombay, 1969, p. 255.
8. Robert Hogan : *Arthur Miller* : Minneapolis, University of Minnesota Press, 1964, p. 32.
9. Arthur Miller : Introduction to the *Collected Plays,* Allied, 1973, pp. 47-49.
10. Barbara Gelb : Question, *"Am I my Brother's Keeper?", The New York Times,* Sunday, November 19, 1964.
11. Quoted by Gilman : "The Drama is Coming Now", *The Modern American Theatre,* p. 165.
12. *Ibid.,* p. 165.

Bibliography

Primary Sources : Books by Arthur Miller

1.A. *The Pussycat and the Expert Plumber who was a Man* (in one Hundred-non-Royalty Radio Plays). ed. William Korlenko, New York, 1941.

Grandus and the Statue, (in Radio Drama in Action), ed. Erik Barnouw, New York, 1944.

The Story of Ous, (in Radio's Best Plays), ed. Joseph Liss, New York, 1947.

Situation Normal, New York, Reynal and Hitchcock, 1944.

A Man Who Had All the Luck, in Cross section, ed. Edwin Seaver, New York, 1944.

Focus, New York : Renal and Hitchcock, 1945.

An Enemy of the People, New York, 1951.

All My Sons, New York, 1957.

Death of a Salesman, Viking, 1949.

The Crucible, Collected Plays, Viking, 1957.

A Memory of Two Mondays, Collected Plays, Viking, 1957.

A View From the Bridge (A Play in Two Acts), Viking, 1960.

The Misfits, New York, 1961.

After the Fall, Viking, 1964.

Incident at Vichy, Viking, 1965.

The Price, Viking, 1968.

The Creation of the World and Other Business, Viking, New York, 1973.

The Ride Down Mt. Morgan, Viking, 1991.

1.B : **Articles by Arthur Miller :**

"Brewed in the Crucible", *The New York Times*, (March 9, 1958).

"The Shadows of the Gods", A critical view of the American Theatre, Harper's 217 (Aug. 1958).

"The Family in Modern Drama", *Times Literary Supplement*, Nov. 25, 1965.

"Tragedy and the Common Man," *New York Times*, Februrary, 1949 II.

"What Makes Play Endure?" *New York Times*, Sunday, January 24, 1971.

Guardian, 25th Feb. 1960.

New York Times, Sunday, Aug. 15, 1965.

"Journey to the Crucible : *New York Times*, February, 1953.

"Foreword to After the Fall", *The Saturday Evening Post*, 237, Feb. 1, 1964.

The New York Times, Sept. 25, 1955.

"With Respect for Her Agony But with Love", (Miller's reply to criticism of After the Fall as Autobiography, *Life*, 56, Feb. 7, 1964.

"After the Fall : An Author's View", *New Haven Register*, April 25, 1965.

Guardian, 23 Jan. 1965.

"The Playwright and the Atomic World", *Colorado Quarterly*, 5 Autumn, 1956.

Introduction to A View From the Bridge, (Two Act Version), New York : Compass, 1960.

"On Recognition", *Michigan Quarterly Review*, 2 (Autumn 1963).

"Written in Prison", *Encounter*, June 30, 1968.

"Many Writers : Few Plays", *The New York Times*, Aug. 10, 1952.

"The Salesman Has a Birthday", *New York Times*, Feb. 5, 1950, Sec. II.

"Broadway From O' Neill to Now", *The New York Times*, Dec. 21, 1969.

The Measure of Things in Man, Theatre 4 : The American Theatre, 1970-71.

"On True Identity", *New York Magazine*, April 13, 1975.

Preface to Adaptation of Henrik Ibsen's An *Enemy of the People*, New York, Viking, 1951.

"The American Theatre", *Holiday*, Jan. 17, 1955.

"On Contemporary Theatre", *Michigan Quarterly Review*, 6 Summer 1964.

On Social Plays, from the original edition of A View from the Bridge (New York, Viking, 1955).

"Man and Words in Prison", *New York Times*, Oct. 16, 1971.

1.C : Interviews :

Allsop Kenneth : "A Conversation with Arthur Miller", *Encounter*, 13 (July 1959).

Anon : "Arthur Miller Ad-Libs on Elia Kazan", *Show* , 2 (Jan. 1964).

Carlisle, Olga : "Arthur Miller : An Interview", *The Paris Review*, 10 (Summer 1966).

Carlisle, Olga and Styron, Rose : "Arthur Miller : An Interview", *The Paris Review*, 10 (Summer 1966).

Corrigan, Robert W. : "Interview : Arthur Miller", Michigan *Quarterly Review*, 13 (Fall 1974).

Gelb, Barbara : :Question : Am I My Brother's Keeper?", *The New York Times*, Sunday, Nov. 29, 1964.

Gelb Phillip : "Morality and Modern Drama", *Educational Theatre Journal*, Oct. 10, 1958.

Collub, Christian Albrecht. : "Interview with Arthur Miller", *Michigan Quarterly Review*, 16 (Spring 1977).

Lamos, Mark : "An Afternoon with Arthur Miller", *The Sunday Statesment*, July, 1987.

Martin, Robert A. : "Arthur Miller-Tragedy and Commitment", *Michigan Quarterly Review*. (Summer, 1969).

---------------- : "The Creative Experience of Arthur Miller : An Interview", *Educational Theatre Journal*, 21 (Oct. 1969).

Martin, Robert A. and Meyer, : "Arthur Miller on Plays and Playwrighting. An Interview", *Modern*

Richard D. *Drama*, 19 (Dec. 1976).

Lewis, Peter : "A Review of The Ride Down Mt. Morgan", *The Sunday Times,* London, Jan. 4, 1992.

Loughlin, Richard L. : "Tradition and Tragedy in All My Sons". *English Record 14.* No. 5, 1964.

Williams, Raymond: "The Realism of Arthur Miller", *Critical Quarterly,* (Summer, 1949).

Hawkins, William : "Death of a Salesman : Powerful Tragedy", *The Critical Review,* No. 9, 1949.

2. Secondary Sources : Scholarship and Criticism

Bentley, Eric : *The Modern Theatre.* A study of Dramatists and the Drama, Robert Hale Ltd., Bedford Square, London, 1948.

________ : *The Playwright as Thinker,* New York, 1957.

Boulton, Marjorie : *The Anatomy of Drama,* Routledge and Kegan Paul Ltd., London, 1946.

Broussard, Louis : *American Drama* (Contemporary Allegory from O' Neill to Williams), University of Oklahoma Press, 1962.

Brown, John Russel: and Harris, Bernard, ed. *American Theatre.* Edward Arnold, London, 1967

Rierman, Judah, Hart, James and Johnson, Stanley : *The Dramatic Experience,* Englewood Cliffs, N.L., 1958.

Brustein, Robert : *The Theatre of Revolt,* Little Brown and Co., Boston, 1964.

Barnish L. Valerie : *"The Crucible",* Methuen Paperbaeks Ltd., London, 1979.

Calderwood, James L. and Toliver, Harold E. (ed.) : *Perspectives on Drama,* New York, Oxford University Press, 1968.

Corrigan, Robert W. (ed.) : *Arthur Miller* (Twentieth Century Views), Prentice-Hall, INC, New Jersey, 1969.

Chase, Richard : *Quest For Myth,* Baton Rouge,

Louisiana State University Press, 1949.

Clurman, Harold : *Arthur Miller*: Themes and Variations, Theatre I, New York : Hill and Wange, Inc., 1964.

Downer, Allen,S.(ed): *American Drama and Its Critics*, University of Chicago Press, 1965.

——————— : *The American Theatre* (Voice of American Forum Lectures), Washington D.C., 1967.

——————— : *Recent American Drama* (Minnesota, 1961).

Dusenbury, L. Winifred : *The Theme of Loneliness in American Drama,* University of Florida Press, Cainsville, 1967.

Freedom, Morris : *American Drama in Social Context,* Southern Illinois University Press, 1971.

Gascoigne, Bamber : *Twentieth Century Drama,* Hutchinson, London, 1962.

Gassner, John : *Masters of the Drama,* D. Publication, Inc., 1954.

Gassnor, John (ed.): *From Henrik Ibsen to Eugene Ionesoc,* Third College Edition, New York, The Dryden Press, 1952.

Gassner, John : *Theatre at the Crossroads,* New York, 1960.

Gassner, John (ed.) : *Directions in Modern Theatre,* Holt, Rinehart and Winston, Inc., New York, 1966.

Gould, Gean : *Modern American Playwrights,* Popular Prakashan, Bombay, 1969.

Hopper, Stanley. (ed.) : *Spiritual Problems in Contemporary Literature* NWK., Harper & Bros., 1952.

Hogan, Robert : *Arthur Miller; University Minnesota, Press, Minneapolis, 1964;*

Huftel, Sheila : *Arthur Miller : The Burning Glass,* The Citadel Press, New York, 1965.

Kernan B. Alvin (ed.) : *The Modern American Threatre,* New Jersey, 1967.

Krutch, J.W. : *The American Drama Since 1918,* Brazillar, 1957.

__________ : *Modernism in Modern Drama,* Ithaca, NY. Cornell University Press, 1953.

Lewis, Allan : *American Plays and Playwrights of the Contemporary Theatre,* Crown Publishers, New York, 1965.

Lumley, Frederick : *New York Trends in 29th Century Drama,* New York, OUP, 1967.

Miller, Arthur : *Collected Plays* (with an Introduction), Allied, New Delhi, 1978.

Martin, James J. (ed.) : *Critical Essays on Arthur Miller,* Boston, G.K. Hall, 1970.

Millet, Fred B. : *Contemporary American Authors,* G., Harrap & Co., London, 1940.

Moss, Leonard : *Arthur Miller,* Twayne Publishers, Inc., New York, 1967.

Mottram, Eric : *The Development of a Political Dramatist American Theatre,* Stratford-Upon-Avon Studies, 1967.

Nadden, David (Ed.) : *American Drama, American Nightmares,* Carbondale, 1970.

Murthy, Rama V. : *An Expressionistic Drama,* Doaba House, Delhi, 1970.

Murray, Edward : *Arthur Miller,* F.U. Publishing Co., New York, 1967.

Nelson, Benjamin : *Arthur Miller, Portrait of a Playwright,* London, 1970.

Nicoll, Allardyce : *World Drama,* Harcourt Brace & Co., New York, 1950.

Nicoll, Allardyce : *The Theatre and Dramatic Theory,* London, 1962.

O'Hara, Frank : *Today in American Drama,* Chicago, 1939.

Pradhan, N.S. : *Modern American Drama,* Arnold Heinemann, New Delhi, 1978.

Steinberg, M.W. (ed.) : *Aspects of Modern Drama,* New York, 1960.

Steiner, George : *The Death of Tragedy,* London, 1961.

Weales, Gerald : *American Drama Since World War II,* Harcourt Brace & Co., Inc., New York, 1962.

Welland, Dennis : *Arthur Miller,* Oliver & Boyd Edinburgh,1961.

Warshaw, Robert : *The Immediate Experience,* New York, Doubleday, 1962.

Williams, Raymond: *Drama From Ibsen to Eliot,* Chatto and Windus, London, 1954.

Wilson, Garff B. : *Three Hundred Years of American Drama and Theatre,* University of California, Berkley, 1959.

Wright, George T. (ed.) : *Seven American Stylists From Poe to Mailer,*University of Minnesota, 1973.

(b) Periodicals Consulted :

Anon : "Arthur Miller in the Crucible" (Film Version). *Audience,* 2 (July-Aug. 1972).

Atkinson, Brooks : 'At the Theatre', *The New York Times,* Jan. 23, 1953.

Baxaundall, Lee : "Arthur Miller still the Innocent", *Encore,* XI May-June, 1964.

Bentley, Eric : "Theatre", *New Republic,* XXXIII Dec. 1955.

Bentley, Eric : "The Innocence of Arthur Miller (From Eric Bentley's What is Theatre?", Incorporating *The Theatre Event and Other Reviews,* 1944-1967, New York, Athenian, 1968.

Bigaby, C.W.E. : "The Fall and After Arthur Miller's Confession", *Modern Drama,* (Sept. 1964).

Clurman, Harold : "Arthur Miller : Themes and Variations", *Theatre I,* New York, Hill & Wang, Inc., 1964.

Curtis, Penelop : "The Crucible", *The Critical Review,* No. 8, 1965.

Findlater, Richard : "No Time for Tragedy", *The Twentieth Century,* Vol. 161, No. 959 (Jan. 1957).

Gelb, Barbara : "Question "Am I My Brother's Keeper"?", *The New York Times,* Sunday, Nov. 2nd, 1964.

Gunj, Arthur : "The Silence of Arthur Miller", *Drama,* Vol. 32, Feb. 1963.

Herne, James A. : "Art's for Truth Sake in Drama", Reprinted from *Arena,* XVIII, 1897.

Hewes, Henry : "Arthur Miller's Cosmic Chuckles", *Saturday Review,* I : 57, Jan. 1973.

Hobson, Harold : "Fair Play, Arthur Miller, The Crucible", *The Sunday Times* (London, Nov. 14, 1954).

Hawkins, William : "Death of a Salesman : Powerful Tragedy", *The Critical Review,* No.9, 1949.

Herr, Walter F. : "The Crucible", *New York Herald Tribune,* Jan. 23, 1953.

Loughlin, L. Richard : "Trradition and Tragedy in All My Sons", *English Record,* 14 No. 3, 1964.

Lewis, Peter : "A Review of the Ride Down Mt. Morgan", *The Sunday Times,* London, Jan. 4, 1992.

Levin, David : "The Crucible in Retrospect", *The New England Quarterly,* XXVIII, Dec. 1955.

Lowenthal, L.D. : "Arthur Miller's Incident at Vichy : A Sartean Interpretation", *Modern Drama,* March, 1975.

Lamos, Mark : "An Afternoon with Arthur Miller", *The Sunday Statesman,* July 12, 1987.

Martin, R.A. : "Arthur Miller and the Meaning of Tragedy", *Modern Drama,* 13 (May 1970).

——————— : "Arthur Miller : Tragedy and Commitment", *Michigan Quak Review,* 8, (Sept. 1969).

Prudho, John : "Arthur Miller and the Tradition of Tragedy", *English Studies,* Vol. 43, No. 5, Oct. 1962.

Schomach, Murray: "Miller Still a Salesman for a Changing Theatre", *The New York Times.*

Seager, Allan : "The Creative Agony of Arthur Miller", *Esquire,* 52 (October, 1959).

Shipley, Joseph I : "Arthur Miller, New Melodrama is not what it seems to be", *The Leader,* XXXVI (Feb. 1953).

Steppart, Michael P. : "Self choice and Aesthetic Despair in Arthur Miller and Tennessee Williams", The *Literary Criterion,* 1985.

Warshaw, Robert : "The Liberal Conscience in the Crucible", *Commentary XV,* March 1953.

Worsley, T.C. : "American Tragedy", *The New Statesmen* and Nation, Aug. 23, 1958.

Index

A

Absence of love, 167
A Doll's House, 25
A Dream Play, 41, 190
Adam and Eve, 171–72
After the Fall, 153, 185, 203, 215
Theme, 157
Comment, 159
Allegoric pattern, 34, 40, 63
Allegory of Quest meaning, 209
Alfierie, 153
All My Sons, 35, 46–47, 70–81, 195, 210
Analysis, 47
Biblical parallel, 47–50
idea, 52, 214
quality, 70
sub-plot, 70
characters, 74
plot, 75, 197
premier, 82
central conflict, 91
tragic drama, 196
America
Post World War I, 23
of 17th century, 212
American
novel/drama, 34, 38
drama
aspect, 57
after 1920s, 61
money ethos, 166
playwrights, 40–41, 44, 63
A Memory of Two Mondays, 134, 201, 213
plot, 140–43
comment, 142
appeal, 146
An Enemy of the People, 26, 72, 210
Arnold, 37
Art/Philosophy, 217
Aristotle's idea
of tragic hero, 128
of poeties, 152
Artand
on metaphysical play, 38
A View from the Bridge, 46, 53, 150, 202
protagonist, 146, 214
tragedy, 150

B

Barry, Philip, 62

Biblical parallels (Miller), 47
Brand, 25
Brech, Bertolt, 33
Broussard Louis, 63
Brustein, 39

C

Cain and Abel, 172
Camino, 63
Capitalism, 23
Chekhov, 31–32
Collected Plays (Miller), 128
  Introduction, 181
Common man (Miller), 107

D

Dataists, 23
Darwin, 20
  formula of evolution, 37
Death of a Salesman, 52, 57–58, 64, 182, 192, 199, 211
  Protagonists, 92
  American Myth, 95
  Original title, 97
  Preface, 98
  House in, 192
Democratic Dispensation beginning, 18
Dialogues, (Miller), 185
Dialectical Materialism, 37
Drama concept (Miller on), 179
Dream (theme), 64

E

Eliot, T.S., 62
Ethical responsibility, 211
Everyman theme, 114
Evil, 101
Experiment Age, 24
Existentialists, 36
Expressionists/Expressionism, 24, 35–36, 41–42, 45, 113, 187
  hallmark, 113
  Miller's experiment, 183
  /Realism—plays with, 191

F

Father-Son antagonism, 210
First World War, 23
  Post, 98
Flash back/Recall in Plays, 190
Flaubert, 32
Freud, 37
From Mom to Midnight, 190

G

Gassier John, 33
Gilman, Richard, 38–39
Ghosts, 19, 25–26

H

Here Come the Clouns, 61
Hero (Creating of), 43
Human
  Behaviour-principles, 121
  hate mechanism, 160

I

Ibsen Henrik, 18–19, 23, 26
  in modern drama, 25
  influence on Miller, 83

Identity Crisis/Search
in *All My Sons*, 91
Millers Plays, 206
Incestuous desire portrayal, 151
Incident at Vichy, 159, 185, 204, 215–16
theme, 162–63, 204
insight, 164
Individual-Society Relationship, 212

J

Jazz age, 23
J.B., 61
Jesus (characterization of), 20

L

Life of Christ, 20

M

Macbeth, 42
Macleish, Archibald, 60
Man
God relationship, 171
Man relationship, 171
Marx, Karl, 20
Married, 27
Masters of the Drama, 33
Maupassaut, 32
Medieval Plays, 188
Metaphysical Plays, 36
Metaphors, 185
Miller, Arthur, 35, 45
plays, 45
attitude, 59
social drama, 84
Death of a Salesman, 95
concern, 209
on drama perspective, 179
play contradiction, 184
contribution to American Drama, 195
position in theatre, 196
Modern
drama, 21
society image, 21
Moral
debt, 167
issues/morality, 200, 202, 210
Mother Courage, 33
Mother Germany, 33
Munich uprising, 23
Myth in drama, 170

N

Naturalism/Supernaturalism, 20
Naturalistic Style, 22, 28
Nietzsche, 21

O

Old Testament parallel (*All my sons*), 47–50
One speaking character, 24
O'Neill, Eugene works, 30–31, 55

P

Parables/fables, 45, 201
Passions elemental, 28
Peer Gynt, 27
Pirandello, Luigi, 28
work, 29

Political theatre decade, 23
Popkin, Henry, 45
Problems of Individual, 211
Prometheus, 42
Prophetic theatre, 210

Q

Quest (Millers), 216
Questioning of past ideologies, 40

R

Radical revolution failure, 20
Realistic
  style, 22, 187
  theatre, 44, 188
  /rhetorical style, 183, 187
Reversal and discovery (Miller's headling of), 186
Romanticism, 17
Rousseau age of, 17
Russian realism, 31

S

Salem witch trials, 120, 127, 199
Second World War, 24
Shakespeare, 42
Shaw, Bernard, 29–30
Sherwood, Robert E., 56
Socio-Political Revolution, 20
Society's evils
  Miller exploration, 80
Social consciousness/responsibility (Miller), 80–88
Son-Father relationships, 205
Sophoclean balance, 32
Strindberg, August, expressionism, 23, 26–28, 41, 63, 187, 191
Struggle in success, 212
Symbolic structural, verbal technique, 185

T

The Adding Machine, 190
The Book of Genesis, 47
The Creation of World and Other Business, 169
The Crucible, 35, 47, 53, 119, 182–83, 212
  tragedy, 123–24, 126, 213
  ending, 130
  criticism, 130
  aspects, 134
  climax, 136
  subject, 199
The Father, 27
The Caucasian Circle of Chalk, 33
The Hairy Ape, 35, 62
The Dance of Death, 41
The Man who had all the Luck, 69, 73, 76, 181, 212
  plot, 71
  flaws, 77
The Misfits, 64, 206
The Pillars of Society, 19, 25
The Petrified Forests, 56, 62
The Price, 165, 205
The Ride Down Mt Mogan, 175
The Skin of Our Teeth, 190
The Wild Duck, 26
Thirties (theatre during), 24
Tragedy (Miller), 107, 123–24
Tragic Drama (*All My Sons*), 196

U

Uncommon Motives, 186

V

Voltaire, 17

W

Warshaw, Robert on *The Crucible*, 135
Wilde, Oscar, 29
Williams, 56–57, 59
    Plays, 57
Witch Hunts, 122
Women (role of), 176

Y

Yeats, 25